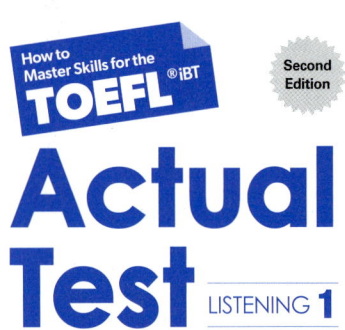

Publisher Kyudo Chung
Editor Inpyo Hong
Authors Michael A. Putlack, Stephen Poirier, Will Link
Proofreader Michael A. Putlack
Designers Minji Kim, Hyounju Yoon

First Published in March 2008 By Darakwon, Inc.
Second edition first published in September 2025 by Darakwon, Inc.
Darakwon Bldg., 211, Munbal-ro, Paju-si, Gyeonggi-do 10881
Republic of Korea
Tel: 02-736-2031 (Ext. 250)
Fax: 02-732-2037

Copyright © 2008 Darakwon, 2025 Darakwon

All rights reserved. No part of this publication may be reproduced, stored in a retrieval system, or transmitted in any form or by any means, electronic, mechanical, photocopying or otherwise, without the prior consent of the copyright owner. Refund after purchase is possible only according to the company regulations. Contact the above telephone number for any inquiries. Consumer damages caused by loss, damage, etc. can be compensated according to the consumer dispute resolution standards announced by the Korea Fair Trade Commission. An incorrectly collated book will be exchanged.

ISBN 978-89-277-8106-6 14740
978-89-277-8105-9 14740 (set)

www.darakwon.co.kr

Photo Credits
Shutterstock.com

Components Main Book / Answer Key / Free MP3 Downloads
7 6 5 4 3 2 1   25 26 27 28 29

Table of Contents

Actual Test 01 009

Actual Test 02 027

Actual Test 03 045

Actual Test 04 063

Actual Test 05 081

Actual Test 06 099

Actual Test 07 117

Actual Test 08 135

INTRODUCTION

1 Information on the TOEFL® iBT

A The Format of the TOEFL® iBT

Section	Number of Questions or Tasks	Timing	Score
Reading	**20 Questions** • 2 reading passages – with 10 questions per passage – approximately 700 words long each	35 Minutes	30 Points
Listening	**28 Questions** • 2 conversations – 5 questions per conversation – 3 minutes each • 3 lectures – 6 questions per lecture – 3-5 minutes each	36 Minutes	30 Points

Speaking	**4 Tasks**
	• 1 independent speaking task
	– 1 personal choice/opinion/experience
	– preparation: 15 sec. / response: 45 sec.
	• 2 integrated speaking tasks: Read-Listen-Speak
	– 1 campus situation topic
	   reading: 75-100 words (45 sec.)
	   conversation: 150-180 words (60-80 sec.)
	– 1 academic course topic
	   reading: 75-100 words (50 sec.)
	   lecture: 150-220 words (60-120 sec.)
	– preparation: 30 sec. / response: 60 sec.
	• 1 integrated speaking task: Listen-Speak
	– 1 academic course topic
	   lecture: 230-280 words (90-120 sec.)
	– preparation: 20 sec. / response: 60 sec.
		17 Minutes	30 Points

Writing	**2 Tasks** • 1 integrated writing task: Read-Listen-Write – reading: 230-300 words (3 min.) – lecture: 230-300 words (2 min.) – a summary of 150-225 words (20 min.) • 1 academic discussion task – a minimum 100-word essay (10 min.)	30 Minutes	30 Points

B What Is New about the TOEFL® iBT?

- The TOEFL® iBT is delivered through the Internet in secure test centers around the world at the same time.
- It tests all four language skills and is taken in the order of Reading, Listening, Speaking, and Writing.
- The test is about 2 hours long, and all of the four test sections will be completed in one day.
- Note taking is allowed throughout the entire test, including the Reading section. At the end of the test, all notes are collected and destroyed at the test center.
- In the Listening section, one lecture may be spoken with a British or Australian accent.
- There are integrated tasks requiring test takers to combine more than one language skill in the Speaking and Writing sections.
- In the Speaking section, test takers wear headphones and speak into a microphone when they respond. The responses are recorded and transmitted to ETS's Online Scoring Network.
- In the Writing section, test takers must type their responses. Handwriting is not possible.
- Test scores will be reported online. Test takers can see their scores online 4-8 business days after the test and can also receive a copy of their score report by mail.

2 Information on the Listening Section

The Listening section of the TOEFL® iBT measures test takers' ability to understand spoken English in English-speaking colleges and universities. This section has 2 conversations that are 12-25 exchanges (about 3 minutes) long and 3 lectures that are 500-800 words (3-5 minutes) long. Each conversation is followed by 5 questions and each lecture by 6 questions. Therefore, test takers have to answer 28 questions in total. The time allotted to the Listening section is 36 minutes, including the time spent listening to the conversations and lectures and answering the questions.

A Types of Listening Conversations and Lectures

- Conversations
  - Between a student and a professor or a teaching assistant during office hours
  - Between a student with a person related to school services such as a librarian, a housing director, a bookstore employee, etc.

- Lectures
  - Monologue lectures delivered by a professor unilaterally
  - Interactive lectures with one or two students asking questions or making comments
    cf. One lecture may be spoken with a British or Australian accent.

B Types of Listening Questions

Type 1 Gist-Content Questions

Gist-Content questions cover the test taker's basic comprehension of the listening passage. While they are typically asked after lectures, they are sometimes asked after conversations as well. These questions check to see if the test taker has understood the gist of the passage. They focus on the passage as a whole, so it is important to recognize what the main point of the lecture is or why the two people in the conversation are having a particular discussion. The test taker should therefore be able to recognize the theme of the lecture or conversation in order to answer this question correctly. On occasion, the test taker is asked to identify two correct answers to a single question.

Type 2 Gist-Purpose Questions

Gist-Purpose questions cover the underlying theme of the passage. While they are typically asked after conversations, they are sometimes asked after lectures as well. Because these questions focus on the purpose or theme of the conversation or lecture, they begin with the word "why." They focus on the conversation or lecture as a whole, but they are not concerned with details; instead, they are concerned with why the student is speaking with the professor or employee or why the professor is covering a specific topic.

Type 3 Detail Questions

Detail questions cover the test taker's ability to understand facts and data that are mentioned in the listening passage. These questions most commonly appear after lectures; however, they also come after conversations, especially when the conversations are about academic topics. Detail questions require the test taker to listen for and remember details from the passage. The majority of these questions concern major details that are related to the main topic of the lecture or conversation rather than minor ones. However, in some cases when there is a long digression that is not clearly related to the main idea, there may be a question about the details of the digression. On occasion, the test taker is asked to identify two correct answers to a single question. These questions may also appear as charts.

Type 4 Understanding Function Questions

Understanding Function questions cover the test taker's ability to determine the underlying meaning of what has been said in the passage. This question type often involves replaying a portion of the listening passage. There are two types of these questions. Some ask the test taker to infer the meaning of a phrase or a sentence. Thus the test taker needs to determine the implication—not the literal meaning—of the sentence. Other questions ask the test taker to infer the purpose of a statement made by one of the speakers. These questions specifically ask about the intended effect of a particular statement on the listener.

Type 5 Understanding Attitude Questions

Understanding Attitude questions cover the speaker's attitude or opinion toward something. These questions may appear after both lectures and conversations. This question type often involves replaying a portion of the listening passage. There are two types of these questions. Some ask about one of the speaker's feelings concerning something. These questions may check to see whether the test taker understands how a speaker feels about a particular topic, if a speaker likes or dislikes something, or why a speaker might feel anxiety or amusement. The other category asks about one of the speaker's opinions. These questions may inquire about a speaker's degree of certainty. Others may ask what a speaker thinks or implies about a topic, person, thing, or idea.

Type 6 Understanding Organization Questions

Understanding Organization questions cover the test taker's ability to determine the overall organization of the passage. These questions almost always appear after lectures. They rarely appear after conversations. These questions require the test taker to pay attention to two factors. The first is the way that the professor has organized the lecture and how the professor presents the information to the class. The second is how individual information given in the lecture relates to the lectures as a whole. To answer these questions correctly, the test taker should focus more on the presentation and the professor's purpose in mentioning the facts rather than the facts themselves.

Type 7 Connecting Content Questions

Connecting Content questions almost exclusively appear after lectures, not after conversations. These questions measure the test taker's ability to understand how the ideas in the lecture relate to one another. These relationships may be explicitly stated, or the test taker may have to infer them from the words that are spoken. The majority of these questions concern major relationships in the passage. These questions also commonly appear in passages in which a number of different themes, ideas, objects, or individuals are being discussed.

Type 8 Making Inference Questions

Making Inferences questions cover the test taker's ability to understand implications made in the passage and to come to a conclusion about what these implications mean. These questions appear after both conversations and lectures. These questions require the test taker to hear the information being presented and then to make conclusions about what the information means or what is going to happen as a result of that information.

Actual Test
LISTENING 1

01

TOEFL LISTENING

Listening Section Directions

This section measures your ability to understand conversations and lectures in English.

The Listening section is divided into separately timed parts. In each part, you will listen to 1 conversation and 1 or 2 lectures. You will hear each conversation or lecture only **one** time.

After each conversation and lecture, you will answer questions about it. The questions typically ask about the main idea and supporting details. Some questions ask about a speaker's purpose or attitude. Answer the questions based on what is stated or implied by the speakers.

You may take notes while you listen. You may use your notes to help you answer the questions. Your notes will not be scored.

If you need to change the volume while you listen, click on the **Volume** icon at the top of the screen.

In some questions, you will see this icon: 🎧 This means that you will hear, but not see, part of the question.

Some of the questions have special directions. These directions appear in a gray box on the screen.

Most questions are worth 1 point. If a question is worth more than 1 point, it will have special directions that indicate how many points you can receive.

A clock at the top of the screen will show you how much time is remaining. The clock will not count down while you are listening. The clock will count down only while you are answering the questions.

PART 1 Conversation

1 What problem does the student have?
- Ⓐ She never received a syllabus for the class.
- Ⓑ Her paper was on an incorrect topic.
- Ⓒ She is going to get a zero on her report.
- Ⓓ She requires more time to finish her work.

2 According to the professor, what should the student's paper be on?
- Ⓐ The differences between some celestial bodies
- Ⓑ The characteristics of Saturn and Jupiter
- Ⓒ An upcoming lunar eclipse that will take place
- Ⓓ The different effects of lunar eclipses on the Earth

3 What can be inferred about the professor?
- Ⓐ He does not get involved in his students' lives.
- Ⓑ He likes to give unsolicited advice to students.
- Ⓒ He is always willing to give extensions on projects.
- Ⓓ He feels that students should not trust one another.

4. Listen again to part of the conversation. Then answer the question.
   What is the purpose of the professor's response:
   - Ⓐ To chastise the student for trusting his friend
   - Ⓑ To ask the student to stop meeting a person
   - Ⓒ To insist that the student think about friendship
   - Ⓓ To advise the student not to be friends with a person

5. Listen again to part of the conversation. Then answer the question.
   What does the professor mean when he says this:
   - Ⓐ The student has an interesting way with words.
   - Ⓑ The student's statement is not strong enough.
   - Ⓒ He does not fully agree with the student.
   - Ⓓ The student's paper was the worst of the semester.

PART 1 Lecture

American History

The Neutrality Act

6 What is the lecture mainly about?

- Ⓐ The historical reasons for American neutrality in World War II
- Ⓑ The root causes that led to the beginning of hostilities in World War II
- Ⓒ The methods the United States used to supply the Allies during the war
- Ⓓ The factors that caused the United States to involve itself in foreign affairs

7 How does the professor organize the lecture?

- Ⓐ By asking a question and then providing answers to it
- Ⓑ By examining an event and the results of this event
- Ⓒ By explaining his theory by going from the present to the past
- Ⓓ By giving some possible results of various past actions

8 According to the professor, what factor was decisive in causing the United States to go to war in 1917?

- Ⓐ The need to help the British and the French defeat Germany
- Ⓑ The desires of the industrialists to make higher profits
- Ⓒ The fears of the government about joining the League of Nations
- Ⓓ The threat of German submarine attacks on American shipping

9 According to the professor, what resulted from the Neutrality Acts?
Click on 2 answers.
- Ⓐ England and France received supplies from the United States.
- Ⓑ Americans could not travel on ships of countries at war.
- Ⓒ Countries had to repay their loans from World War I to the United States.
- Ⓓ Countries at war could not borrow money from the United States.

10 Listen again to part of the lecture. Then answer the question.
What does the professor mean when he says this:
- Ⓐ The United States supports the United Nations' enforcement of peace.
- Ⓑ Even with American support, the United Nations cannot enforce peace.
- Ⓒ Peace can be enforced by the United States with the United Nations' help.
- Ⓓ Even with support, peace cannot be enforced by international bodies.

11 Listen again to part of the lecture. Then answer the question.
What does the professor mean when he says this:
- Ⓐ Roosevelt might have had a hard time declaring war on Germany.
- Ⓑ The Germans should have made another treaty with Japan.
- Ⓒ The world was lucky that Germany declared war on the United States.
- Ⓓ Hitler's biggest mistake came in declaring war on the United States.

PART 2 Conversation

TOEFL
LISTENING

1 Why does the student visit the financial aid office?
- Ⓐ To attempt to renew her need-based scholarship
- Ⓑ To complain about the recent increase in tuition
- Ⓒ To ask about the possibility of additional assistance
- Ⓓ To request some additional forms for financial aid

2 According to the student, what kind of financial aid is she currently receiving? Click on 2 answer choices.
- Ⓐ An athletic scholarship
- Ⓑ A need-based scholarship
- Ⓒ A student loan
- Ⓓ An academic scholarship

3 What can be inferred about the student?
- Ⓐ She was raised in a poor environment.
- Ⓑ She is currently majoring in science.
- Ⓒ She prefers to spend her time studying.
- Ⓓ She expects to withdraw from school.

4 What will the student probably do next?
- Ⓐ Provide the man with more financial details
- Ⓑ Complete the form for a student loan
- Ⓒ Apply for some academic scholarships
- Ⓓ Request more information on financial aid

5 Listen again to part of the conversation. Then answer the question.
What is the purpose of the student's response:
- Ⓐ To express her doubt at the possibility of the man's idea succeeding
- Ⓑ To state that she believes the man's suggestion is excellent
- Ⓒ To encourage the man to give her a different suggestion
- Ⓓ To declare that she is not very interested in the man's suggestion

Geography

6 What is the lecture mainly about?
- Ⓐ How people navigate from point to point by using imaginary lines
- Ⓑ The roles of time and time measurement on different parts of the Earth
- Ⓒ How people use imaginary lines to regulate time and navigation
- Ⓓ The history of how latitude and longitude were measured and used

7 According to the professor, for what do people mainly use lines of latitude and longitude?
- Ⓐ To know where they are and where they are going
- Ⓑ To determine how quickly they can complete a trip
- Ⓒ To judge when the summer begins in each hemisphere
- Ⓓ To describe where the tropical and frigid zones are

8 How does the professor organize the lecture?
- Ⓐ By discussing a fact and the reasons for it
- Ⓑ By pointing out the history of a certain fact
- Ⓒ By dividing discussion on a fact into two main parts
- Ⓓ By examining the parts of a specific fact in detail

9 In the lecture, the professor discusses imaginary lines in places around the Earth. Indicate to which imaginary line the following statements are related.

Click in the correct box for each sentence.

	Latitude	Longitude
1 It includes the International Date Line.		
2 It was difficult for people to determine in the past.		
3 It begins at the equator.		
4 It was easy to determine based on the sun's position over the horizon.		

10 Listen again to a part of the lecture. Then answer the question.

Why does the professor say this:

- Ⓐ Time is not related to navigation even though they have similar terms.
- Ⓑ Time and navigation use the same terms but should not be confused.
- Ⓒ The degrees of a circle are not the same as the measurements used on a clock.
- Ⓓ There is often confusion between time and navigation terms.

11 Listen again to part of the lecture. Then answer the question.

What does the professor imply when she says this:

- Ⓐ There were similar problems with clocks on land.
- Ⓑ Clocks of the time relied on metal springs.
- Ⓒ The metal of the age was too poor for clockworks.
- Ⓓ Clocks were accurate on land but not at sea.

Chemistry

12 What aspect of chemistry does the professor discuss?
- (A) The discovery of the parts of the atom
- (B) The Greek view of the elements
- (C) The structure and history of the periodic table
- (D) The noble gases and the rare earth elements

13 According to the professor, what determines the isotope of an element?
- (A) The atomic weight
- (B) The number of protons
- (C) The number of neutrons
- (D) The number of electrons

14 How does the professor organize the lecture?
- (A) By dividing the discussion into two main parts
- (B) By making a point and then providing an example
- (C) By discussing the points in chronological order
- (D) By providing a conclusion and then the reasons for it

15 In the lecture, the professor explains the makeup of the atom. Indicate to which part of the atom the following statement is related.

Click in the correct box for each sentence.

	Proton	Neutron	Electron
1 Has no electric charge			
2 Bonds with other elements to make molecules			
3 Determines an element's atomic number			
4 Is not located in the nucleus			

16 What does the professor imply about the periodic table of the elements?
- Ⓐ It will remain the same.
- Ⓑ It will increase in size.
- Ⓒ It will be reorganized.
- Ⓓ It will be replaced.

17 Listen again to a part of the lecture. Then answer the question.
What does the professor imply when he says this: 🎧
- Ⓐ Most of what he will say was discovered by people a long time ago.
- Ⓑ The majority of students should already have learned the material.
- Ⓒ The students should have read their books before coming to class.
- Ⓓ The students need to pay closer attention than they did in high school.

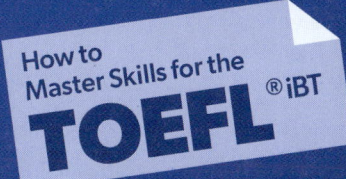

Actual Test
LISTENING 1

02

TOEFL LISTENING

Listening Section Directions

This section measures your ability to understand conversations and lectures in English.

The Listening section is divided into separately timed parts. In each part, you will listen to 1 conversation and 1 or 2 lectures. You will hear each conversation or lecture only **one** time.

After each conversation and lecture, you will answer questions about it. The questions typically ask about the main idea and supporting details. Some questions ask about a speaker's purpose or attitude. Answer the questions based on what is stated or implied by the speakers.

You may take notes while you listen. You may use your notes to help you answer the questions. Your notes will not be scored.

If you need to change the volume while you listen, click on the **Volume** icon at the top of the screen.

In some questions, you will see this icon: 🎧 This means that you will hear, but not see, part of the question.

Some of the questions have special directions. These directions appear in a gray box on the screen.

Most questions are worth 1 point. If a question is worth more than 1 point, it will have special directions that indicate how many points you can receive.

A clock at the top of the screen will show you how much time is remaining. The clock will not count down while you are listening. The clock will count down only while you are answering the questions.

1 Why does the student visit the professor's office?
- Ⓐ To introduce herself to him
- Ⓑ To discuss a recent grade
- Ⓒ To get some tips for her report
- Ⓓ To learn her TA's office number

2 What is the professor's attitude toward the student?
- Ⓐ He is somewhat domineering.
- Ⓑ He is inconsiderate of her feelings.
- Ⓒ He is interested in her progress.
- Ⓓ He is willing to accept her beliefs.

3 What does the professor imply about Tom Watkins?
- Ⓐ He will help the student improve her grade.
- Ⓑ Tom can teach better than the professor himself.
- Ⓒ He is always available when people need him.
- Ⓓ He has assisted many other students in the past.

4 What will the student probably do next?
- Ⓐ Go to the third floor
- Ⓑ Resubmit her exam
- Ⓒ Prepare for her paper
- Ⓓ Call Tom in his office

5 Listen again to part of the conversation. Then answer the question.
Why does the student say this:
- Ⓐ She wants the professor to show her Tom's office.
- Ⓑ She would like the professor to grade her test again.
- Ⓒ She thinks the professor should raise her grade a few points.
- Ⓓ She is hoping to receive some tips on studying properly.

6 What aspect of the eye does the professor mainly discuss?
- Ⓐ The way in which the lens is affected by the pupil and the iris
- Ⓑ Typical problems with people's vision and their causes
- Ⓒ Differences between nearsightedness and farsightedness
- Ⓓ Misconceptions of myopia, hyperopia, and astigmatism

7 According to the professor, what is the function of the iris?
- Ⓐ It is the opening which allows light into the eye.
- Ⓑ It covers and protects the eye from hazardous substances.
- Ⓒ It focuses light images and projects them onto the retina.
- Ⓓ It controls the movement and size of the pupil.

8 According to the professor, what is one way astigmatism can affect vision?
- Ⓐ The eye is shorter than normal and hinders focusing.
- Ⓑ The image comes into focus before it reaches the retina.
- Ⓒ The eye becomes confused by multiple focal points.
- Ⓓ The individual can see distant objects very clearly.

9 Are the following characteristics of astigmatism, myopia, or hyperopia?
Click in the correct box for each sentence.

	Astigmatism	Myopia	Hyperopia
1 Another word for this condition is farsightedness			
2 Images close up can be read easily.			
3 The cornea is shaped like an egg.			
4 The image comes into focus before the retina.			

10 What does the professor imply about myopia?
 Ⓐ It occurs when the eyeball is too long in size.
 Ⓑ It is not as serious a condition as hyperopia.
 Ⓒ It is capable of getting worse with age.
 Ⓓ It is caused when the cornea is misshapen.

11 Listen again to part of the lecture. Then answer the question.
What does the professor imply when she says this: 🎧
 Ⓐ She expects the students to realize vision is more complex.
 Ⓑ She wants her students to understand bones do not aid in vision.
 Ⓒ She thinks her explanation is too complex for the students.
 Ⓓ She hopes the students can retain the information she has given them.

PART 2 Conversation

1. What do the speakers mainly discuss?
   - Ⓐ How to be safe in a laboratory environment
   - Ⓑ Various accidents that occurred in the past
   - Ⓒ The location of the laboratory's safety gear
   - Ⓓ The need to wear protective gear at all times

2. Why does the student visit the laboratory?
   - Ⓐ To do a makeup assignment
   - Ⓑ To fulfill his professor's request
   - Ⓒ To conduct his experiment
   - Ⓓ To put on some protective gear

3. According to the woman, why must the student always wear protective gear?
   - Ⓐ To avoid harming himself while in the lab
   - Ⓑ To prevent spreading chemicals to others
   - Ⓒ To keep chemicals from escaping the lab
   - Ⓓ To stop various chemicals from exploding

4 What must the student wear in the laboratory at all times?
Click on 2 answers.
- Ⓐ A mask
- Ⓑ Gloves
- Ⓒ Boots
- Ⓓ A lab coat

5 Listen again to part of the conversation. Then answer the question.
What does the woman imply when she says this: 🎧
- Ⓐ Some chemicals can cause upset stomachs.
- Ⓑ She does not want to take the man to the hospital.
- Ⓒ Previous students have consumed some chemicals.
- Ⓓ The student could die if he eats any of the chemicals.

History

6 What is the main topic of the lecture?

- Ⓐ How the slave trade negatively affected African society
- Ⓑ The importance and value of African oral traditions
- Ⓒ The way in which modern music mirrors slave songs
- Ⓓ Why African stories relied on repetition and rhythm

7 According to the professor, where do most forms of modern music originate?

- Ⓐ From the oral tradition of slave songs and stories
- Ⓑ From earlier forms of jazz and the blues
- Ⓒ From the West African storytellers of the 1500s
- Ⓓ From slave songs present in the West Indies

8 According to the professor, what did the oral tradition of slaves accomplish?

- Ⓐ It allowed them to reunite with members of their families.
- Ⓑ It helped them become more efficient workers in the fields.
- Ⓒ It gave them a form of entertainment without instruments.
- Ⓓ It provided them with a form of secret communication.

9 How does the professor organize the information about African oral traditions that he presents to the class?

  Ⓐ By starting at the beginning and moving forward
  Ⓑ By tracing its roots back into the past
  Ⓒ By comparing the oral traditions to modern styles
  Ⓓ By randomly giving specific examples to the students

10 What can be inferred about early slaves?

  Ⓐ They were resilient human beings.
  Ⓑ They were tormented and brutalized.
  Ⓒ They picked up the English language easily.
  Ⓓ They lost their connection with their homelands.

11 Listen again to part of the lecture. Then answer the question.
What can be inferred about the student when she says this: 🎧

  Ⓐ She is unhappy because she knows her answer is incorrect.
  Ⓑ She is excited that she was able to come up with the answer.
  Ⓒ She is regretful that the answer she gives is a tragic one.
  Ⓓ She is sorry that she did not let the professor finish the question.

Anthropology

12 What is the main topic of the lecture?

- Ⓐ The specific area of Africa where the first humans originated
- Ⓑ The journeys of early humans out of Africa and into Australia
- Ⓒ The earliest movements of humans as tracked by scientists
- Ⓓ Why early humans chose to move eastward instead of westward

13 According to the professor, why are the Niah Caves important?

- Ⓐ Fossil evidence places humans there forty thousand years ago.
- Ⓑ They show that the first humans may have lived in India.
- Ⓒ Early humans crossed land bridges to reach these caves.
- Ⓓ The fossils found there predate the ones found in Australia.

14 According to the professor, how has scientists' understanding of human migration improved?

- Ⓐ Carbon dating has become more precise over the past few years.
- Ⓑ Scientists in different disciplines confirm one another's findings.
- Ⓒ Scientists now know that early humans were able to push over the Himalayas.
- Ⓓ Artifacts reveal more than ever due to advances in genetic modification.

15 How is the discussion organized?
- Ⓐ The professor covers points chronologically.
- Ⓑ The professor presents a cause and then discusses an effect.
- Ⓒ The professor relates dates in order of their importance.
- Ⓓ The professor states the pros and cons of certain events.

16 In the lecture, the professor describes the early humans in Central Asia and North America. Indicate with which continent the following statements are connected.

Click in the correct box for each sentence.

	Central Asia	North America
[1] Humans most likely scaled massive mountains to enter this region.		
[2] Humans probably arrived there around 30,000 years ago.		
[3] Humans might have used a land bridge to get there.		
[4] Humans arrived there between twenty and fifteen thousand years ago.		

17 Listen again to part of the lecture. Then answer the question.

What does the professor imply when he says this: 🎧
- Ⓐ The sea provided food for early humans.
- Ⓑ The western Mediterranean was inaccessible.
- Ⓒ Early humans did not know how to build boats.
- Ⓓ Early groups often became lost while traveling.

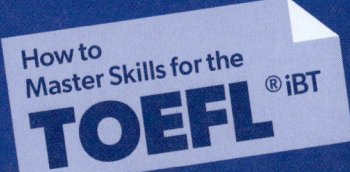

Actual Test
LISTENING 1

03

TOEFL LISTENING

Listening Section Directions

This section measures your ability to understand conversations and lectures in English.

The Listening section is divided into separately timed parts. In each part, you will listen to 1 conversation and 1 or 2 lectures. You will hear each conversation or lecture only **one** time.

After each conversation and lecture, you will answer questions about it. The questions typically ask about the main idea and supporting details. Some questions ask about a speaker's purpose or attitude. Answer the questions based on what is stated or implied by the speakers.

You may take notes while you listen. You may use your notes to help you answer the questions. Your notes will not be scored.

If you need to change the volume while you listen, click on the **Volume** icon at the top of the screen.

In some questions, you will see this icon: 🎧 This means that you will hear, but not see, part of the question.

Some of the questions have special directions. These directions appear in a gray box on the screen.

Most questions are worth 1 point. If a question is worth more than 1 point, it will have special directions that indicate how many points you can receive.

A clock at the top of the screen will show you how much time is remaining. The clock will not count down while you are listening. The clock will count down only while you are answering the questions.

1 What are the speakers mainly discussing?
  Ⓐ Problems with some of the residential assistants
  Ⓑ Issues that students living in a dormitory have
  Ⓒ The need to renovate some of the school's buildings
  Ⓓ Dormitory life and why it is so unpleasant

2 According to the student, who does he represent?
  Ⓐ Students in his major
  Ⓑ Students in their first year of study
  Ⓒ Students living at their homes
  Ⓓ Students living in a dormitory

3 Why does the woman mention the company that handles cleaning?
  Ⓐ To claim that it is doing the work that it should
  Ⓑ To provide the student with a contact name and number
  Ⓒ To suggest that it is not fulfilling its obligations
  Ⓓ To refute the point that the student is making

4. What can be inferred about the woman?
   Ⓐ She will meet some residential assistants soon.
   Ⓑ She is hearing complaints for the first time.
   Ⓒ She is uninterested in the student's comments.
   Ⓓ She does not have the power to help the student.

5. Listen again to part of the conversation. Then answer the question.
   What is the purpose of the woman's response:
   Ⓐ To say that a topic is not up for discussion
   Ⓑ To state that she will look into a matter
   Ⓒ To request more information from the student
   Ⓓ To respond negatively to the student's request

Geography

6 What aspect of deltas does the professor mainly discuss?
- Ⓐ The method of their formation
- Ⓑ The wildlife that lives there
- Ⓒ Ancient delta formations
- Ⓓ Humans that live there

7 The shape of a river delta is mainly influenced by which of the following?
Click on 2 answers.
- Ⓐ The tide where the river ends
- Ⓑ The speed of the river
- Ⓒ The type of sediment in the river
- Ⓓ The speed of the wind

8 How does the professor organize the lecture?
- Ⓐ She talks about different geographic regions and the deltas found there.
- Ⓑ She explains an important point about deltas and then provides examples.
- Ⓒ She discusses all aspects of deltas and then provides some examples.
- Ⓓ She examines the history of deltas as well as man's influence on them.

9 What is the professor's opinion of the flooding of rivers?
- Ⓐ Humans should do more to control it.
- Ⓑ Flooding is almost always beneficial to people.
- Ⓒ There is nothing people can do about floods.
- Ⓓ It can be both positive and negative.

10 What does the professor imply about the Aswan Dam?
- Ⓐ It has been a great benefit to Egypt.
- Ⓑ It has managed to control flooding.
- Ⓒ It was an ecological mistake.
- Ⓓ It has totally destroyed the delta.

11 Listen again to part of the lecture. Then answer the question.
What does the professor mean when she says this: 🎧
- Ⓐ The Nile delta is still increasing in size despite the waves.
- Ⓑ The waves have had a small influence on the Nile delta.
- Ⓒ The Nile delta has remained the same size for many years.
- Ⓓ The Nile delta is shrinking in size as a result of the waves.

1 Why does the student visit the professor?

Ⓐ She wants to discuss her work at the autism center.
Ⓑ She is having difficulty choosing her thesis topic.
Ⓒ She needs to choose a different subject for a paper.
Ⓓ She wants to discuss some different ways to treat autism.

2 What danger does the professor warn the student about concerning the field of study she is interested in?

Ⓐ Too many people are writing about that field these days.
Ⓑ There are very few resources concerning her field of study.
Ⓒ Her field of study is open to prejudicial opinions if she is not careful.
Ⓓ There is a lot of controversy with many conflicting opinions in the field.

3 What is the professor's attitude toward the mothers raising autistic children alone?

Ⓐ He finds this to be very curious.
Ⓑ He is somewhat disinterested.
Ⓒ He feels sympathetic toward them.
Ⓓ He is heartbroken by the thought.

4. What can be inferred about the professor?
   Ⓐ He has some knowledge in the area the student wants to research.
   Ⓑ He is the school's leading expert on the student's area of study.
   Ⓒ He is not really interested in the topic the student likes.
   Ⓓ He is a single parent trying to raise his own autistic child.

5. Listen again to part of the conversation. Then answer the question.
   What does the professor mean when he says this:
   Ⓐ The student should make sure she understands everything she observes.
   Ⓑ The student should not make any judgments until her study is complete.
   Ⓒ The student must learn as much about autism as she can before beginning.
   Ⓓ The student needs to keep her opinions to herself throughout her research.

World History

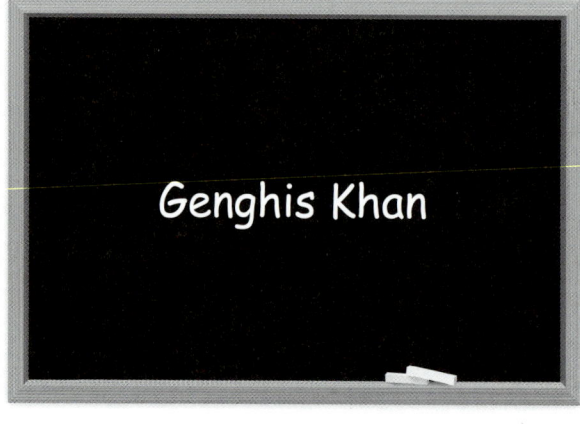

6 Which aspect of Genghis Khan's life does the professor mainly discuss?
Click on 2 answers.
- Ⓐ His military conquests
- Ⓑ How he decided on his successor
- Ⓒ His rise to power
- Ⓓ His childhood

7 According to the professor, what dramatic event played a crucial role in Genghis Khan's development as a warrior?
- Ⓐ The death of his father at an early age
- Ⓑ The killing of his elder half-brother
- Ⓒ The kidnapping of his wife by another tribe
- Ⓓ His victory over the other Mongol tribes

8 Why does the professor discuss Genghis Khan's early life in great detail?
- Ⓐ To show how Genghis Khan became a warrior
- Ⓑ To depict vividly how harsh Mongol life was
- Ⓒ To explain why there were succession problems
- Ⓓ To demonstrate that he was a lawless criminal

9. In the lecture, the professor describes some important events in Genghis Khan's life. Indicate during which part of his life the following events took place.

Click in the correct box for each sentence.

	Childhood	Middle Years	Later Life
1 The kidnapping of his wife			
2 The conquest of Mongol tribes			
3 The succession crisis			
4 The killing of his half-brother			

10. What can be inferred about why Genghis Khan's two eldest sons hated each other?

Ⓐ Genghis Khan made his second son the successor to his empire.
Ⓑ The second son thought that he was Genghis's real first son.
Ⓒ The first son was an alcoholic and wasted everyone's wealth.
Ⓓ Genghis Khan failed to teach them to respect each other.

11. Listen again to part of the lecture. Then answer the question.

Why does the professor say this:

Ⓐ To show that the Mongols were merciful in their dealings with people
Ⓑ To imply that mercy was not a part of the Mongol warrior code
Ⓒ To emphasize that the Mongols treated some people very harshly
Ⓓ To say that people showed mercy to the Mongols who surrendered

Physiology

12 What is the main topic of the lecture?

Ⓐ Bloodletting and the history of blood transfusions
Ⓑ The history of blood transfusions and how plasma is used
Ⓒ The history of blood transfusions and different blood types
Ⓓ Different blood types and how plasma is used by doctors

13 According to the professor, what is true about blood transfusions?

Ⓐ They were very common in the seventeenth century.
Ⓑ They saved many soldiers' lives during wartime.
Ⓒ They helped lengthen George Washington's life.
Ⓓ They did not become very common until recently.

14 What is the professor's opinion of donating blood?

Ⓐ People should be paid to do it.
Ⓑ It can give some people deadly diseases.
Ⓒ It is something people should be forced to do.
Ⓓ It is completely safe for people to do.

15 What can be inferred about people in the United States?

- (A) They are mostly unaware of their blood type.
- (B) They donate blood more than ever before.
- (C) The majority of them have RH negative blood.
- (D) Fewer than ten percent of them have AB blood.

16 Listen again to part of the lecture. Then answer the question.
What does the professor imply about bloodletting when she says this:

- (A) It was once considered a good medical practice.
- (B) It was an unusual medical treatment of the time.
- (C) It is still an accepted medical practice.
- (D) It is similar to how people donate blood.

17 Listen again to part of the lecture. Then answer the question.
What does the professor mean when she says this:

- (A) There are enough donors with O negative blood.
- (B) Transfusions with O negative blood are the best type.
- (C) There are not enough blood donors in the country.
- (D) There is not enough O negative blood donated.

How to Master Skills for the TOEFL® iBT

Actual Test
LISTENING 1

04

TOEFL LISTENING

Listening Section Directions

This section measures your ability to understand conversations and lectures in English.

The Listening section is divided into separately timed parts. In each part, you will listen to 1 conversation and 1 or 2 lectures. You will hear each conversation or lecture only **one** time.

After each conversation and lecture, you will answer questions about it. The questions typically ask about the main idea and supporting details. Some questions ask about a speaker's purpose or attitude. Answer the questions based on what is stated or implied by the speakers.

You may take notes while you listen. You may use your notes to help you answer the questions. Your notes will not be scored.

If you need to change the volume while you listen, click on the **Volume** icon at the top of the screen.

In some questions, you will see this icon: 🎧 This means that you will hear, but not see, part of the question.

Some of the questions have special directions. These directions appear in a gray box on the screen.

Most questions are worth 1 point. If a question is worth more than 1 point, it will have special directions that indicate how many points you can receive.

A clock at the top of the screen will show you how much time is remaining. The clock will not count down while you are listening. The clock will count down only while you are answering the questions.

PART 1 Conversation

1 What are the speakers mainly discussing?
- Ⓐ The man's weekly eating patterns
- Ⓑ The meal plan options available
- Ⓒ The cost of various meal plans
- Ⓓ The university's rules on meal plans

2 According to the student, how often does he eat in the cafeteria?
- Ⓐ About seven times a week
- Ⓑ Around ten times a week
- Ⓒ About fourteen times a week
- Ⓓ Around twenty-one times a week

3 What is the woman's attitude toward the student?
- Ⓐ She is somewhat condescending.
- Ⓑ She is particularly disinterested.
- Ⓒ She is rather informative.
- Ⓓ She is overly excited.

4 What will the student probably do next?
- Ⓐ Ask for a refund on his meal plan
- Ⓑ Consider all of his options first
- Ⓒ Sign up for the fourteen-a-week plan
- Ⓓ Ask the employee for some more information

5 Listen again to part of the conversation. Then answer the question. What can be inferred from the student's response to the woman: 🎧
- Ⓐ He is the most interested in that meal plan.
- Ⓑ He has no interest in that specific meal plan.
- Ⓒ He will sign up for that meal plan in the future.
- Ⓓ He will consider signing up for that meal plan.

American History

6 What aspect of transatlantic flight does the professor mainly discuss?
- Ⓐ The difficulties involved in such an ambitious undertaking
- Ⓑ A description of the planes involved and their impact on the future
- Ⓒ Why Pan Am decided to take the risk of beginning these routes
- Ⓓ A comparison between Clippers and modern jet aircraft like the Boeing 747

7 According to the professor, what was Pan Am's intention with Clippers?
Click on 2 answers.
- Ⓐ To dominate the North Atlantic market
- Ⓑ To provide top-notch service to wealthy passengers
- Ⓒ To create a global network of flights
- Ⓓ To be the first airline to fly across the oceans

8 What is the professor's attitude toward Clippers?
- Ⓐ He is impressed by the first-class travel they provided.
- Ⓑ He feels that they traveled too slowly.
- Ⓒ He believes the price of tickets on them was too high.
- Ⓓ He thinks they were not very advanced for their time.

9 What does the professor imply about modern commercial aircraft?
- Ⓐ They are much larger than the first commercial airplanes that crossed the oceans.
- Ⓑ They have minimal comfort in contrast to the luxurious Clipper aircraft.
- Ⓒ They borrow many of the early design features from Pan Am planes.
- Ⓓ They are not as safe as the Clippers because they do not have floating capabilities.

10 Are the following characteristics of the Clipper aircraft or the Boeing 747?
Click in the correct box for each sentence.

	Clipper Aircraft	Boeing 747
① Its fare equaled that of the Concorde.		
② It was put into service in the late 1960s		
③ It was used to transport soldiers.		
④ It had a larger seating capacity.		

11 Listen again to part of the lecture. Then answer the question.
What does the professor imply when he says this: 🎧
- Ⓐ Borders became more transparent with the advent of transoceanic flights.
- Ⓑ Pan Am's early Clipper service helped begin to unite the people of the world.
- Ⓒ Most countries were completely isolated from one another before Clipper flights.
- Ⓓ For the first time, individuals were able to visit foreign lands with few impediments.

Literature

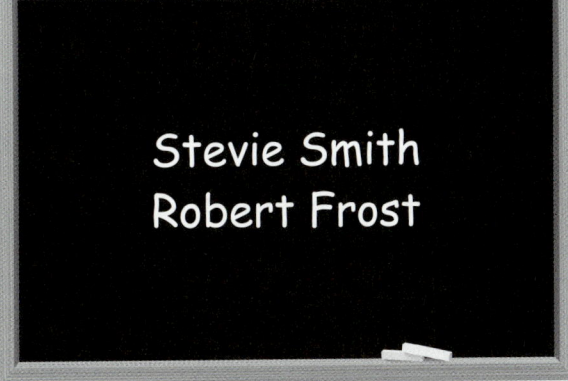

Stevie Smith
Robert Frost

12 What aspect of the two poems does the professor mainly discuss?

　Ⓐ How they both deviate from each other in terms of their themes
　Ⓑ How each one's tone reveals the exploration of the surface of things
　Ⓒ A comparison of life and death symbols and their importance
　Ⓓ The way in which a person's initial perceptions can be deceptive

13 According to the professor, why does Smith have the deceased individual on the beach speak?

　Ⓐ To suggest that the person has not actually perished
　Ⓑ To reveal the latent spiritual motif of the poem
　Ⓒ To indicate how observers misinterpreted the warning signs
　Ⓓ To show how the person was in trouble his entire life

14 What does the professor imply about the individual's death in *Not Waving, But Drowning*?

　Ⓐ He could have been saved if his signal had been accurately interpreted by bystanders.
　Ⓑ It was no accident that the person drowned because of his serious internal problems.
　Ⓒ People should pay closer attention to the intentions of others, not simply their actions.
　Ⓓ While clearly a tragedy, humans should try to respect the forces of nature more.

15 According to the professor, which path in life does Frost believe people should take?
- Ⓐ A way that contains the most obstacles and hurdles
- Ⓑ The one that does not have a clear ending or course
- Ⓒ A direction that gives a person the option to change his mind
- Ⓓ A proven course that is comfortable and simple to track

16 Are the following characteristics of Smith's or Frost's poem?
Click in the correct box for each sentence.

	Smith	Frost
① The narrator commits suicide.		
② Uncertainty helps the narrator decide.		
③ It is the longer poem of the two.		
④ It contains multiple stanzas.		

17 Listen again to part of the lecture. Then answer the question.
What does the professor imply when she says this: 🎧
- Ⓐ She thinks the students are making it difficult on themselves.
- Ⓑ She believes even a complex operation could not save the person.
- Ⓒ She worries that the students are looking too deeply into the meaning.
- Ⓓ She cannot understand why the class does not agree with her explanation.

PART 2 Conversation

TOEFL
LISTENING

1 Why does the student visit the professor?
- Ⓐ To get the professor's permission for something
- Ⓑ To enroll in one of the professor's classes
- Ⓒ To ask about taking Professor Marrone's class
- Ⓓ To find out if she can take a full load of classes

2 What is the student's opinion of her Latin class?
- Ⓐ She thinks it is very straightforward.
- Ⓑ She dreads having to take it.
- Ⓒ She thoroughly enjoys the class.
- Ⓓ She thinks she can handle the work.

3 Why does the professor mention Professor Davidson?
- Ⓐ To say that he does not easily hand out high grades
- Ⓑ To state that the student will enjoy his class
- Ⓒ To remind the student that he teaches Latin classes
- Ⓓ To inquire as to whether the student has taken him before

4 Listen again to part of the conversation. Then answer the question.
What does the professor imply when he says this: 🎧
  Ⓐ He got excellent grades in her science classes.
  Ⓑ His major back in college was one of the sciences.
  Ⓒ He did not get high grades in his science classes.
  Ⓓ He wishes that he could take a science class again.

5 Listen again to part of the conversation. Then answer the question.
What does the professor imply when he says this: 🎧
  Ⓐ The student has done a satisfactory job.
  Ⓑ The student has thought about her classes a lot.
  Ⓒ The student needs to reconsider her new idea.
  Ⓓ The student will probably do very well in her class.

Physiology

6 What is the main topic of the lecture?
  Ⓐ A comparison between skeletal muscle and smooth muscle
  Ⓑ How voluntary and involuntary muscles are different from one another
  Ⓒ The differences between the body's three different muscle types
  Ⓓ The process of muscle movement originating from the ANS and the SNS

7 According to the professor, what is a distinguishing characteristic of skeletal muscles?
  Ⓐ They connect to bones via separate connective tissues like ligaments and tendons.
  Ⓑ They are controlled by the somatic nervous system and are involuntary.
  Ⓒ They line the outer edge of major respiratory organs such as the lungs.
  Ⓓ They comprise small muscle groups of the human body and are banded together.

8 Why does the professor mention the biceps?
  Ⓐ To show how muscles always pull and never push
  Ⓑ To indicate what striated muscles look like
  Ⓒ To explore the major muscles of the arm
  Ⓓ To give an example of a major skeletal muscle

9 What does the professor imply about smooth muscle?
- Ⓐ It is usually found in thin layers between tendons and bone.
- Ⓑ It is critical to the human body because it aids in breathing.
- Ⓒ It is essentially controlled by the autonomic nervous system.
- Ⓓ It contains a heavy network of blood vessels to keep it functioning.

10 According to the professor, what is true of cardiac muscle?
- Ⓐ It is a combination of both smooth and skeletal muscle.
- Ⓑ It is more similar to skeletal muscle than smooth muscle.
- Ⓒ It requires electric impulses from the brain and the ANS to function.
- Ⓓ It lines the walls of the stomach, which makes digestion more efficient.

11 Are the following characteristics of cardiac, smooth, or skeletal muscles?
Click in the correct box for each sentence.

	Cardiac	Smooth	Skeletal
① The latissimus dorsi is an example of this type.			
② This type of muscle lines the intestines.			
③ This is the most abundant muscle in the human body			
④ This type of muscle is a mix of the other two.			

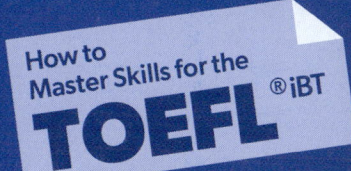

Actual Test
LISTENING 1

05

TOEFL LISTENING

Listening Section Directions

This section measures your ability to understand conversations and lectures in English.

The Listening section is divided into separately timed parts. In each part, you will listen to 1 conversation and 1 or 2 lectures. You will hear each conversation or lecture only **one** time.

After each conversation and lecture, you will answer questions about it. The questions typically ask about the main idea and supporting details. Some questions ask about a speaker's purpose or attitude. Answer the questions based on what is stated or implied by the speakers.

You may take notes while you listen. You may use your notes to help you answer the questions. Your notes will not be scored.

If you need to change the volume while you listen, click on the **Volume** icon at the top of the screen.

In some questions, you will see this icon: 🎧 This means that you will hear, but not see, part of the question.

Some of the questions have special directions. These directions appear in a gray box on the screen.

Most questions are worth 1 point. If a question is worth more than 1 point, it will have special directions that indicate how many points you can receive.

A clock at the top of the screen will show you how much time is remaining. The clock will not count down while you are listening. The clock will count down only while you are answering the questions.

PART 1 Conversation

TOEFL
LISTENING

1 What problem does the student have?
- Ⓐ She does not like her room assignment.
- Ⓑ She cannot fit her room key into the lock.
- Ⓒ The room she has is too decrepit.
- Ⓓ Her dormitory room is uninhabitable.

2 Why does the student visit the student housing office?
- Ⓐ To ask for another place to stay
- Ⓑ To make a list of complaints
- Ⓒ To request a transfer to another room
- Ⓓ To demand compensation for her room

3 According to the student, what is wrong with her room?
Click on 2 answer choices.
- Ⓐ It is currently infested with insects.
- Ⓑ It is not large enough for two people.
- Ⓒ It has not been sufficiently cleaned.
- Ⓓ The light in the room will not turn on.

4. What can be inferred about the man?
   - Ⓐ He has handled this kind of problem before.
   - Ⓑ He has a generally unpleasant personality.
   - Ⓒ He knows all of the school's housing policies.
   - Ⓓ He tries to be as thorough as possible in his job.

5. Listen again to part of the conversation. Then answer the question.
   What is the purpose of the student's response:
   - Ⓐ To indicate that there are numerous problems
   - Ⓑ To show that she is not willing to compromise
   - Ⓒ To specify that she needs new accommodations
   - Ⓓ To clarify her previous statement about her room

History

6 What aspect of the Black Death does the professor mainly discuss?

- Ⓐ Its socio-economic impact on fourteenth-century Europe
- Ⓑ The root of its cause and what was done to cure it
- Ⓒ Its onset and how the two strains were able to spread
- Ⓓ Its death toll and how it affected certain populations

7 Why does the professor mention Sicily?

- Ⓐ To claim its population was wiped out by the Black Death
- Ⓑ To name the place where the Black Death entered Europe
- Ⓒ To call it a major port on the Mediterranean Sea
- Ⓓ To say that its people recovered quickly from the Black Death

8 What can be inferred about the pneumonic plague?

- Ⓐ It paled in comparison to the death caused by the bubonic plague.
- Ⓑ It was probably originally spawned by the bubonic plague.
- Ⓒ It proved fatal within a few days to anyone who contracted it.
- Ⓓ It attacked the lymph nodes and the immune system in the human body.

9 According to the professor, how did population affect the spread of the Black Death?
- Ⓐ More densely populated areas allowed it to stay around longer.
- Ⓑ The sparsely populated areas helped the disease spread more quickly.
- Ⓒ It did little to affect its spread because the disease was not contagious.
- Ⓓ Populations big or small had nothing to do with the proliferation of the plague.

10 Are the following characteristics of the bubonic or pneumonic plague?
Click in the correct box for each sentence.

	Bubonic	Pneumonic
1 It had a 100% fatality rate.		
2 It was contracted from rodents.		
3 It was passed from human to human.		
4 It affected a larger portion of the population.		

11 Listen again to part of the lecture. Then answer the question.
What does the professor imply when she says this: 🎧
- Ⓐ Cities were the ideal breeding ground for a plague.
- Ⓑ Cleaner lifestyles could have reduced the devastation.
- Ⓒ The environment was the root of the Black Death.
- Ⓓ Europeans should have put more importance on garbage collection.

1. What are the speakers mainly discussing?
   - Ⓐ The student's attempt to sign up for the professor's class
   - Ⓑ The African-American writer Zora Neale Hurston
   - Ⓒ The student's grades in some classes taken previously
   - Ⓓ The professor's opinion on some classes the student may take

2. According to the professor, what are Dr. Whitlam's classes like?
   Click on 2 answers.
   - Ⓐ They can be difficult for the students.
   - Ⓑ They are full of energy.
   - Ⓒ They are full of class discussions.
   - Ⓓ They are unpopular because of their topics.

3. What does the professor imply about Professor Rice?
   - Ⓐ She is an expert in various Eastern religions.
   - Ⓑ She just became the head of her department.
   - Ⓒ She does not specialize in religions from Africa.
   - Ⓓ She is not one of the more popular professors in the department.

4 According to the professor, what is crucial to a folklore class?
- Ⓐ An exploration of different religious influences on the writers
- Ⓑ A well-structured syllabus that the students can follow
- Ⓒ Readings of one of its major contributors, Zora Neale Hurston
- Ⓓ Other modern examples of literature coming from the South

5 Listen again to part of the conversation. Then answer the question.
Why does the student say this:
- Ⓐ To indicate that the registration policy benefits upperclassmen
- Ⓑ To declare that the class is only popular with juniors and seniors
- Ⓒ To mention that the class will be difficult for freshmen and sophomores
- Ⓓ To encourage the professor to change the school's registration method

Health and Nutrition

6 What is the main topic of the lecture?
- Ⓐ The effects of certain types of insomnia on the human body
- Ⓑ How depression and stress can result in narcolepsy
- Ⓒ The causes of the two major types of sleeping disorders
- Ⓓ Why hypersomnia is more common than types of insomnia

7 According to the professor, what is true about narcolepsy?
- Ⓐ An individual with it gets too much sleep at night.
- Ⓑ It is an uncontrollable urge to fall asleep during the daytime.
- Ⓒ A person with it can only sleep for around five minutes at a time.
- Ⓓ It is typically caused by too much stress, anxiety, or worry.

8 What can be inferred about insomnia?
- Ⓐ If it is not diagnosed early, a person with it could cause an accident.
- Ⓑ A person suffering from it is prone to get illnesses and diseases.
- Ⓒ It is not a very serious issue because it can be cured by medicine easily.
- Ⓓ Drinks with caffeine as well as nicotine are its most common causes.

9 According to the professor, what is a problem with using medication?
Click on 2 answers.
- Ⓐ It can cause addiction in some people.
- Ⓑ It can be too expensive for most people.
- Ⓒ It can often fail to work properly.
- Ⓓ It can have various side effects.

10 Are the following statements consistent with hypersomnia or insomnia?
Click in the correct box for each sentence.

	Hypersomnia	Insomnia
① Melatonin may help with this sleeping disorder.		
② Modifying the circadian rhythm is a good remedy.		
③ A vegetable-rich diet could alleviate the symptoms.		
④ Some extreme forms are passed on genetically.		

11 Listen again to part of the lecture. Then answer the question.
Why does the student say this:
- Ⓐ To apologize to the professor for not paying attention
- Ⓑ To reveal that she was unable to fall asleep the previous night
- Ⓒ To indicate that she is well prepared for the lecture
- Ⓓ To note that she could not sleep because of her studies

Physiology

Endomorph
Mesomorph
Ectomorph

12 What is the lecture mainly about?
- Ⓐ How heredity affects a person's personality
- Ⓑ People's basic somatotypes
- Ⓒ Reasons why body shapes seldom change
- Ⓓ Type A and B personalities

13 According to the professor, what can affect a person's body type?
- Ⓐ The type of diet that the person follows
- Ⓑ The genetics of a specific individual
- Ⓒ The density of one's bones and muscles
- Ⓓ The desire of the person to change

14 What does the professor imply about personalities?
- Ⓐ They always correlate with a person's body type.
- Ⓑ They have no relation to a person's body type.
- Ⓒ In general, certain body types display similar ones.
- Ⓓ In recent studies, personalities change as body types do.

15 According to the professor, what are mesomorphs more prone to do?
   Ⓐ They tend to embrace competition and activity.
   Ⓑ They enjoy eating more than they exercise.
   Ⓒ They might often be lethargic and inactive.
   Ⓓ They usually have more health problems.

16 Are the following characteristics of people with type A or type B personalities?
Click in the correct box for each sentence.

	Type A	Type B
1 They tend to be sensitive.		
2 They are usually highly competitive.		
3 They have a lot of confidence.		
4 They might not like to talk too much.		

17 Listen again to part of the lecture. Then answer the question.
What can be inferred about the professor when he says this: 🎧
   Ⓐ He is shy about having the students critique his body.
   Ⓑ He is worried the students will not participate.
   Ⓒ He is embarrassed about his own body type.
   Ⓓ He is enthusiastic about using himself as an example.

Actual Test

LISTENING 1

06

TOEFL LISTENING

Listening Section Directions

This section measures your ability to understand conversations and lectures in English.

The Listening section is divided into separately timed parts. In each part, you will listen to 1 conversation and 1 or 2 lectures. You will hear each conversation or lecture only **one** time.

After each conversation and lecture, you will answer questions about it. The questions typically ask about the main idea and supporting details. Some questions ask about a speaker's purpose or attitude. Answer the questions based on what is stated or implied by the speakers.

You may take notes while you listen. You may use your notes to help you answer the questions. Your notes will not be scored.

If you need to change the volume while you listen, click on the **Volume** icon at the top of the screen.

In some questions, you will see this icon: 🎧 This means that you will hear, but not see, part of the question.

Some of the questions have special directions. These directions appear in a gray box on the screen.

Most questions are worth 1 point. If a question is worth more than 1 point, it will have special directions that indicate how many points you can receive.

A clock at the top of the screen will show you how much time is remaining. The clock will not count down while you are listening. The clock will count down only while you are answering the questions.

PART 1 Conversation

TOEFL

LISTENING | Questions 1~3 of 11

1 Why did the woman visit the student?
- Ⓐ To talk about the reservation that he made
- Ⓑ To discuss a club that he helps run
- Ⓒ To mention a problem she can help solve
- Ⓓ To find out why he wanted to meet her

2 What can be inferred about the student?
- Ⓐ He was unable to meet the woman yesterday.
- Ⓑ He is currently in his final semester.
- Ⓒ He belongs to the Music Department.
- Ⓓ He is considering becoming a professional actor.

3 In the conversation, the student describes a number of facts about his drama club. Indicate whether each of the following is a fact about the drama club.

Click in the correct box for each sentence.

	Fact	Not a Fact
① The name of the club is the Royal Players.		
② The club has performed a play before.		
③ The club is currently in its second semester.		
④ The club needs help managing the stage.		

4 When does the woman believe would be ideal for the man to make a reservation?
- Ⓐ On a Monday night
- Ⓑ On a Tuesday night
- Ⓒ On a Thursday night
- Ⓓ On a Sunday night

5 What will the student probably do next?
- Ⓐ Visit the woman's office with her
- Ⓑ Confirm his reservation
- Ⓒ Go to the school library
- Ⓓ Attend a rehearsal for a play

Literature

6 What aspect of Poe's short story does the professor discuss?
- Ⓐ Some major themes such as death and revenge
- Ⓑ How the setting is important to the plot
- Ⓒ A comparison of the two main characters
- Ⓓ How symbolism plays a major role in the story's development

7 According to the professor, what is the main difference between Fortunato and Montresor?
- Ⓐ Fortunato has much more wealth than Montresor.
- Ⓑ They attained their societal status in dissimilar ways.
- Ⓒ Montresor is much wiser than the foolish Fortunato.
- Ⓓ Montresor is an executioner while Fortunato is a dupe.

8 According to the professor, how did Fortunato gain his wealth?
- Ⓐ He inherited it from some of his rich ancestors.
- Ⓑ He usurped it from some naïve investors.
- Ⓒ He acquired a lot of money through an accident.
- Ⓓ He built an empire through a lot of hard work.

9 What can be inferred about Montresor?

    Ⓐ He is of a lower status than Fortunato.
    Ⓑ He does not want to reveal who he is.
    Ⓒ He is planning on killing Fortunato.
    Ⓓ He is a thief preparing to rob Fortunato.

10 In the lecture, the professor discusses the characteristics of Fortunato and Montresor. Indicate which character the following statements characterize.

Click in the correct box for each sentence.

	Fortunato	Montresor
① His costume bells jingle when he speaks.		
② He is a member of the nobility.		
③ His ancestors are buried in the catacombs.		
④ He is a member of the nouveau riche.		

11 Listen again to part of the lecture. Then answer the question.

What does the professor imply when he says this: 🎧

    Ⓐ He believes the students are aware of the meaning of catacombs.
    Ⓑ He wishes he could challenge the students to be better in class.
    Ⓒ He wonders whether or not he could have explained it better.
    Ⓓ He thinks the students do not completely understand his lecture.

PART 2 Conversation

TOEFL

LISTENING

1. Why did the professor ask to see the student?
   - Ⓐ To make a suggestion about his final paper topic
   - Ⓑ To look over his class notes from the semester
   - Ⓒ To find out what his paper topic idea is
   - Ⓓ To inquire about what has been bothering him lately

2. What does the professor imply about the student?
   - Ⓐ He allows his mind to wander at times.
   - Ⓑ He does not follow directions very well.
   - Ⓒ He needs to work on his listening skills.
   - Ⓓ He lacks confidence in his writing ability.

3. What happened to the student's text and notes?
   - Ⓐ He lost both of them at the library.
   - Ⓑ He lost them at a restaurant off campus.
   - Ⓒ He let another student borrow them.
   - Ⓓ He left them at a coffee shop on campus.

4. What is the professor's attitude toward the student?
   - Ⓐ She is suspicious of his intentions.
   - Ⓑ She wishes the student would try harder.
   - Ⓒ She is somewhat protective of him.
   - Ⓓ She feels bothered by his lack of common sense.

5. Listen again to part of the talk. Then answer the question.
   What does the professor imply when she says this:
   - Ⓐ She thinks some papers are full of too many grammatical mistakes.
   - Ⓑ She believes students include unimportant information in their papers.
   - Ⓒ She wonders why students wait until the last minute to begin writing.
   - Ⓓ She cannot understand why students do not use outlines for organization.

Geology

6 What aspect of earthquakes does the professor mainly discuss?

- Ⓐ How the study of plate tectonics has revealed their major causes
- Ⓑ The effects they have both above and below the ground
- Ⓒ The difficulty involved in attempting to predict them
- Ⓓ How earthquake forecasts determine when they will occur

7 Why does the professor discuss weather prediction?

- Ⓐ To claim that it is not very accurate nowadays
- Ⓑ To contrast it with earthquake prediction
- Ⓒ To indicate how advanced the technology for it is
- Ⓓ To note that weather influences earthquakes

8 According to the professor, what is the most famous fault in the world?

- Ⓐ The San Andreas Fault
- Ⓑ The Hayward Fault
- Ⓒ The Pacific Fault
- Ⓓ The North American Fault

9 What can be inferred about earthquakes?

Ⓐ They take time to build up before they happen.
Ⓑ Experts cannot accurately guess when they will happen.
Ⓒ Without them, plate tectonics would not exist.
Ⓓ More will occur if scientists drill deep into the ground.

10 In the lecture, the professor describes weather and earthquake forecasts. Indicate which type of forecast the following statements are a description of.

Click in the correct box for each sentence.

	Weather Forecast	Earthquake Forecast
1 It is moderately accurate.		
2 It is almost always completely off.		
3 It uses doppler radar.		
4 Most experts refuse to attempt it.		

11 Listen again to part of the lecture. Then answer the question.
Why does the professor say this:

Ⓐ To show that most earthquakes occur when they are least expected
Ⓑ To note that, one day, earthquake prediction will be an exact science
Ⓒ To reveal the futility of trying to determine when earthquakes will occur
Ⓓ To indicate how little scientists actually know about earthquake formation

American History

Steamboats

12 What aspect of steamboats does the professor mainly discuss?
- Ⓐ The changes they created in the United States
- Ⓑ Two examples of the first successful steamboats
- Ⓒ An explanation of how elaborately they were designed
- Ⓓ Their competition and eventual loss to the railroad

13 According to the professor, what is one reason why steamboats were so successful?
- Ⓐ They were somewhat impervious to fire and other dangers.
- Ⓑ They carried supplies such as sugar and machinery.
- Ⓒ They were able to navigate rivers in either direction.
- Ⓓ They were romanticized by people along the rivers.

14 Why does the professor mention the *Titanic*?
- Ⓐ To show the type of vessels that developed from early steamboats
- Ⓑ To emphasize the sheer extravagance present on some steamboats
- Ⓒ To indicate the excellent engineering associated with both ships
- Ⓓ To note that all great ships must face an end at some juncture

15 According to the professor, why did the railroad replace the steamboat?

   (A) It was more comfortable than river travel.
   (B) It had a more consistent schedule.
   (C) It cost much less to travel on.
   (D) It was less prone to sporadic fires.

16 Are the following characteristics of Captain Fulton or Captain Shreve?
Click in the correct box for each sentence.

	Fulton	Shreve
1 He completed a 1,400-mile trip in three weeks.		
2 His boat suffered from poor mechanics.		
3 He was one of the first to navigate to New Orleans.		
4 He was the captain of the *Washington*.		

17 Listen again to part of the lecture. Then answer the question.
What does the professor imply when she says this:

   (A) Steamboat captains discovered some shortcuts.
   (B) Engineering improved tremendously over the years.
   (C) Trips along the rivers took less time than ever before.
   (D) New navigation techniques were more efficient.

How to Master Skills for the TOEFL® iBT

Actual Test
LISTENING 1

07

TOEFL LISTENING

Listening Section Directions

This section measures your ability to understand conversations and lectures in English.

The Listening section is divided into separately timed parts. In each part, you will listen to 1 conversation and 1 or 2 lectures. You will hear each conversation or lecture only **one** time.

After each conversation and lecture, you will answer questions about it. The questions typically ask about the main idea and supporting details. Some questions ask about a speaker's purpose or attitude. Answer the questions based on what is stated or implied by the speakers.

You may take notes while you listen. You may use your notes to help you answer the questions. Your notes will not be scored.

If you need to change the volume while you listen, click on the **Volume** icon at the top of the screen.

In some questions, you will see this icon: 🎧 This means that you will hear, but not see, part of the question.

Some of the questions have special directions. These directions appear in a gray box on the screen.

Most questions are worth 1 point. If a question is worth more than 1 point, it will have special directions that indicate how many points you can receive.

A clock at the top of the screen will show you how much time is remaining. The clock will not count down while you are listening. The clock will count down only while you are answering the questions.

PART 1 Conversation

TOEFL

LISTENING

1 Why does the student visit the professor?
- Ⓐ To ask a question about a recent lecture
- Ⓑ To talk about a possible research topic
- Ⓒ To discuss his schedule for the next semester
- Ⓓ To inquire about an archaeological dig

2 What does the student want to focus on?
- Ⓐ The archaeology of Greece and Rome
- Ⓑ The archaeology of ancient Egypt
- Ⓒ The archaeology of Central America
- Ⓓ The archaeology of Europe

3 What is the professor's attitude toward the student?
- Ⓐ She is helpful in suggesting ideas to him.
- Ⓑ She is a bit impatient with his indecision.
- Ⓒ She praises him for his hard work.
- Ⓓ She thinks that he is her best student.

4 What will the professor probably do next?
- Ⓐ Write a book list for the student
- Ⓑ Go to the library with the student
- Ⓒ Start preparing for her next class
- Ⓓ Show the student a book in her collection

5 Listen again to part of the conversation. Then answer the question. What does the student mean when he says this:
- Ⓐ He cannot carry all of the books the professor gave him.
- Ⓑ He has to read too many books for his final exams.
- Ⓒ He will read all of the books during summer vacation.
- Ⓓ He does not have enough time to read five books.

Zoology

Scavengers

6 What aspect of scavengers does the professor mainly discuss?
- Ⓐ The places around the world where the majority of them live
- Ⓑ Ways that the majority of them find food to eat
- Ⓒ Various types of them and their consumption methods
- Ⓓ The main differences between scavengers, predators, and prey

7 According to the professor, what is a typical characteristic of a scavenger?
Click on 2 answers.
- Ⓐ An outstanding ability to smell things
- Ⓑ Excellent usage of camouflage
- Ⓒ A powerful digestive system
- Ⓓ Strong teeth and sharp claws or talons

8 Based on the information in the lecture, indicate which statements refer to hyenas or vultures.
Click in the correct box for each sentence.

	Hyenas	Vultures
1 Are protected from bacteria by their bald heads		
2 Are known to hunt other animals in packs		
3 May consume a dead animal together with lions at times		
4 Are able to crack bones open with their teeth		

9 Why does the professor mention marine snow?

- Ⓐ To tell the students how it is created
- Ⓑ To say that it is polluting the oceans
- Ⓒ To claim it sustains entire fish populations
- Ⓓ To state that only crabs and lobsters eat it

10 Why does the professor tell the students about fishermen?

- Ⓐ To mention that scavengers reduce the number of fish they catch
- Ⓑ To complain about some of the fishing methods they use
- Ⓒ To describe what they do when they find carcasses in the water
- Ⓓ To explain how they manage to catch some marine animals

11 According to the professor, how do scavengers benefit their ecosystems?

- Ⓐ They provide nutrients for other animals living nearby.
- Ⓑ They reduce the populations of some animals.
- Ⓒ They remove animals that are carrying diseases.
- Ⓓ They help keep waterways clean and free of carcasses.

1 What are the speakers mainly discussing?
Click on 2 answers.
- Ⓐ Where some reference books are
- Ⓑ The student's book fines
- Ⓒ How to check out books
- Ⓓ Book renewals for students

2 According to the man, what happens if a book is not returned within two weeks of its due date?
- Ⓐ The student must pay for the book in full.
- Ⓑ Late fines double each day the book is not returned.
- Ⓒ The student must pay five dollars per book.
- Ⓓ The student will not be allowed to check out any books.

3 According to the man, why have the late fines for library books increased?
- Ⓐ The university needs funds to build a new library at the junior college.
- Ⓑ Many students have been neglecting to return their books on time.
- Ⓒ The policy was long overdue for an upgrade according to the school.
- Ⓓ Professors complained about not having access to critical historical texts.

4 What will the student probably do next?

- Ⓐ Speak to her professor about a paper extension
- Ⓑ Look in the stacks for the books she needs
- Ⓒ Check two books out from the junior college library
- Ⓓ Return to her dorm room for some cash to pay the fines

5 Listen again to part of the conversation. Then answer the question.
Why does the student say this:

- Ⓐ Her professor will be furious with her.
- Ⓑ She will probably fail her upcoming exam.
- Ⓒ The books are the basis for her homework.
- Ⓓ She has never gotten an F on a paper before.

Engineering

6 What aspect of oceanic cables does the professor mainly discuss?
- Ⓐ How they are important to world communications
- Ⓑ The way in which they are planted in the ocean floor
- Ⓒ Why a trench-digging apparatus sometimes disrupts their functions
- Ⓓ The methods by which cable ships map their placement

7 What does the professor imply about oceanic cables?
- Ⓐ Only a few countries are capable of laying them.
- Ⓑ Laying them on the ocean floor requires advanced technology.
- Ⓒ They often suffer problems that require repairs.
- Ⓓ It can take years to lay them across an entire ocean.

8 According to the professor, what is crucial to the trencher?
- Ⓐ It is able to move independently of the cable ship.
- Ⓑ It uses water to blast away at the soil and sediment.
- Ⓒ Its light weight makes it perfect for building cable trenches.
- Ⓓ Its speed allows it to lay cables in half the time of prior methods.

9 According to the professor, why do oceanic cables not float away before they are buried?

  Ⓐ The trencher keeps them pinned to the ocean floor.
  Ⓑ The cable ship forces the cable down with mechanical arms.
  Ⓒ The cable is filled with some kind of heavy material.
  Ⓓ The cable is displaced over a large area on the seafloor.

10 The professor explains the steps in the process of laying an oceanic cable. Put these steps in order.

Step 1	
Step 2	
Step 3	
Step 4	

  Ⓐ The cable is spooled off the deck of the cable ship.
  Ⓑ The jets of the trencher blast away the seabed.
  Ⓒ The trencher is lowered into the water.
  Ⓓ Engineers map the position of the cable.

11 Listen again to part of the lecture. Then answer the question.
What does the professor imply when she says this: 🎧

  Ⓐ The makeup of the ocean floor often varies.
  Ⓑ The ocean floor is always hard to blast.
  Ⓒ The trencher cannot always cut into the seabed.
  Ⓓ Without different blast settings, the trencher would be useless.

12 What is the main topic of the lecture?

- Ⓐ The formation process of glaciers
- Ⓑ Different kinds of glaciers
- Ⓒ How glaciers can shape the land
- Ⓓ The rapid disappearance of glaciers

13 Based on the information in the lecture, indicate which type of glacier the statements refer to.

Click in the correct box for each sentence.

	Continental Ice Sheets	Ice Caps	Ice Fields
1 Are typically flat in shape			
2 Are only two of them in existence now			
3 Can be found in the Himalayas			
4 May cover entire mountain ranges			

14 What is the professor's attitude toward the student?

- Ⓐ She considers him the class's top student.
- Ⓑ She is impressed with the way he thinks.
- Ⓒ She likes that he read the class material.
- Ⓓ She is impatient with all of his questions.

15 According to the professor, why do ice streams move fast?
Click on 2 answers.
- Ⓐ They can have sediment mixed with their ice.
- Ⓑ They are fairly small in size so are lightweight.
- Ⓒ They descend from the highest mountains at times.
- Ⓓ They may have liquid water flowing beneath them.

16 What can be inferred about outlet glaciers?
- Ⓐ They are not as wide as ice streams.
- Ⓑ They tend to move at slow speeds.
- Ⓒ They are normally found on flat land.
- Ⓓ They can take years to become large.

17 Why does the professor tell the students about their textbooks?
- Ⓐ To tell them to look at some pictures in the books
- Ⓑ To give them a homework assignment
- Ⓒ To say that everyone needs to purchase one
- Ⓓ To name the chapters in it covered by a test

How to Master Skills for the TOEFL® iBT

Actual Test LISTENING 1

08

TOEFL LISTENING

Listening Section Directions

This section measures your ability to understand conversations and lectures in English.

The Listening section is divided into separately timed parts. In each part, you will listen to 1 conversation and 1 or 2 lectures. You will hear each conversation or lecture only **one** time.

After each conversation and lecture, you will answer questions about it. The questions typically ask about the main idea and supporting details. Some questions ask about a speaker's purpose or attitude. Answer the questions based on what is stated or implied by the speakers.

You may take notes while you listen. You may use your notes to help you answer the questions. Your notes will not be scored.

If you need to change the volume while you listen, click on the **Volume** icon at the top of the screen.

In some questions, you will see this icon: 🎧 This means that you will hear, but not see, part of the question.

Some of the questions have special directions. These directions appear in a gray box on the screen.

Most questions are worth 1 point. If a question is worth more than 1 point, it will have special directions that indicate how many points you can receive.

A clock at the top of the screen will show you how much time is remaining. The clock will not count down while you are listening. The clock will count down only while you are answering the questions.

PART 1 Conversation

1. What are the speakers mainly discussing?
   - Ⓐ A topic for the student's next class assignment
   - Ⓑ An argument the student recently read about
   - Ⓒ A paper the student submitted to the professor
   - Ⓓ An essay test that the student just took

2. Why does the professor mention the student's introduction in his paper?
   - Ⓐ To say that it uses an improper quote
   - Ⓑ To state that it is not long enough
   - Ⓒ To praise the way that it was written
   - Ⓓ To ask the student to completely rewrite it

3. What does the professor say about the student's paper?
   Click on 2 answers.
   - Ⓐ It does not contain enough words.
   - Ⓑ It contains some spelling mistakes.
   - Ⓒ It makes a few poor arguments.
   - Ⓓ It needs to include more quotations.

4 What can be inferred about the student's paper?
- Ⓐ It is worth almost half of the grade for the class.
- Ⓑ It must be turned in sometime next week.
- Ⓒ It is about a topic the student is unfamiliar with.
- Ⓓ It is required to be at least ten pages long.

5 Listen again to part of the conversation. Then answer the question.
What does the professor imply when she says this:
- Ⓐ She wants to talk to the student about his paper.
- Ⓑ The student is being impolite by still standing.
- Ⓒ She is not willing to return the student's paper.
- Ⓓ The student did poorly on his recent exam.

Astronomy

6 What is the lecture mainly about?
- Ⓐ The way coronal mass ejections develop
- Ⓑ Solar wind's various effects on the sun
- Ⓒ The discovery and effects of solar wind
- Ⓓ The problems solar wind causes on the Earth

7 How does the professor organize the information about the discovery of solar wind that he presents to the class?
- Ⓐ By discussing it in chronological order
- Ⓑ By mentioning the work of multiple astronomers
- Ⓒ By talking about his contributions to the effort
- Ⓓ By focusing on the discoveries made by space probes

8 Why does the professor mention Eugene Parker?
- Ⓐ To argue that his findings were incorrect
- Ⓑ To say that he discovered coronal mass ejections
- Ⓒ To discuss a theory that he came up with
- Ⓓ To cite a book that he wrote about the sun

9 What can be inferred about slow solar wind?
  Ⓐ It is much more common than fast solar wind.
  Ⓑ It was discovered by Eugene Parker.
  Ⓒ It travels around 400 kilometers per second.
  Ⓓ It forms near the sun's north and south poles.

10 What does the professor imply about Mars?
  Ⓐ There is no magnetosphere protecting it.
  Ⓑ Astronomers believe life once existed on it.
  Ⓒ Its orbit has been changed by solar wind.
  Ⓓ Solar wind has made its surface radioactive.

11 According to the professor, what can happen during powerful solar wind storms?
Click on 2 answers.
  Ⓐ People may be unable to get Internet service.
  Ⓑ Satellites can be forced from orbit down to the Earth.
  Ⓒ Rockets are not able to launch into outer space.
  Ⓓ Navigation systems may not work properly.

History

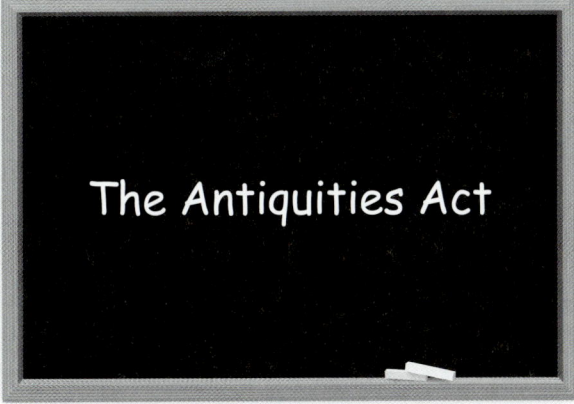

12 What is the lecture mainly about?
- Ⓐ The differences between national parks and monuments
- Ⓑ The Antiquities Act and its importance
- Ⓒ The establishment of the first American national park
- Ⓓ The Grand Canyon and the Statue of Liberty

13 What can be inferred about the creation of national monuments?
- Ⓐ The citizens of the United States can petition for their establishment.
- Ⓑ Congress will continue to maintain and fund them in the future.
- Ⓒ It happens much more quickly than the creation of national parks.
- Ⓓ The president has little control over when and how they are set up.

14 According to the professor, what was the first national monument in the United States?
- Ⓐ The Grand Canyon
- Ⓑ The Statue of Liberty
- Ⓒ Devil's Tower
- Ⓓ Escalante

15 According to the professor, what did President Clinton do?

- Ⓐ He broadened the appeal of monuments in the United States.
- Ⓑ He founded the Northwestern Hawaiian Islands Marine National Monument.
- Ⓒ He established a record number of national monuments.
- Ⓓ He attempted to have the Antiquities Act repealed.

16 In the lecture, the professor discusses U.S. national parks and national monuments. Indicate in which category each of the following statements belongs.

Click in the correct box for each sentence.

	National Parks	National Monuments
1 They can take a long time to be established.		
2 Congress can establish them.		
3 Congress has little control over their creation.		
4 The Antiquities Act is used to establish these.		

17 Listen again to part of the lecture. Then answer the question.

What can be inferred from the professor's response to the student: 🎧

- Ⓐ He wants the students to understand the protective vision of many U.S. presidents.
- Ⓑ He believes that many presidents did not have the best interests of the country in mind.
- Ⓒ He hopes future presidential projects will not be taken advantage of like in the past.
- Ⓓ He thinks the students should realize that many presidents protected land for their own benefit.

PART 2 Conversation

TOEFL
LISTENING

08-04

1 What are the speakers mainly discussing?
- Ⓐ How to form a new club on campus
- Ⓑ Where the student's club should meet
- Ⓒ What the student can do as a club leader
- Ⓓ What kinds of clubs are on campus

2 What is on the list the student gives the woman?
Click on 2 answers.
- Ⓐ Identification numbers
- Ⓑ Home addresses
- Ⓒ Telephone numbers
- Ⓓ Signatures

3 What can be inferred about the woman?
- Ⓐ She just started her first week of work.
- Ⓑ She used to be the president of a student club.
- Ⓒ She will reserve a room for the student soon.
- Ⓓ She will attend a meeting of the student's club.

4 What is the student's attitude toward the woman?
- Ⓐ He feels pleased with the way that she assists him.
- Ⓑ He is disappointed she cannot answer every question.
- Ⓒ He is impressed with her knowledge of the school.
- Ⓓ He feels thankful that she provided some funding for him.

5 Listen again to part of the conversation. Then answer the question.
What does the woman imply when she says this: 🎧
- Ⓐ There are numerous clubs at the school.
- Ⓑ Some clubs only have meetings once a semester.
- Ⓒ She expects few students to request assistance.
- Ⓓ The presidents of most clubs need her help.

History

6 Which aspect of the Bronze Age does the professor mainly discuss?
- Ⓐ Its differences from the Stone Age
- Ⓑ The places it happened
- Ⓒ Its primary features
- Ⓓ The inventions made during it

7 Why does the professor tell the students about their midterm papers?
- Ⓐ To note that he will return them soon
- Ⓑ To state his pleasure with the ones he has read
- Ⓒ To say that they must be ten pages long
- Ⓓ To remind the students about the due date

8 What can be inferred about the Sumerians?
- Ⓐ They entered the Stone Age before 3000 B.C.
- Ⓑ They were the largest of all Stone Age civilizations.
- Ⓒ They were the first people to invent writing.
- Ⓓ They traded with people in the Mediterranean region.

9 Why does the professor mention Cornwall?
- Ⓐ To call it a center of trade in the Bronze Age
- Ⓑ To point out that tin and copper were mined there
- Ⓒ To say it was where people first made bronze
- Ⓓ To claim that a great city was established there

10 According to the professor, what was a main feature of the Bronze Age?
Click on 2 answers.
- Ⓐ The practice of warfare
- Ⓑ The development of writing systems
- Ⓒ The discovery of agriculture
- Ⓓ The increase of urbanization

11 What is the professor's attitude toward the student?
- Ⓐ He is happy with her performance on a test.
- Ⓑ He is excited about her questions.
- Ⓒ He is pleased with her thought process.
- Ⓓ He is satisfied with her response to his question.

How to Master Skills for the TOEFL® iBT

Second Edition

Actual Test

Answers
Scripts
Explanations

LISTENING 1

DARAKWON

ACTUAL TEST 01

p.009

Answers

PART 1

1	Ⓑ	2	Ⓐ	3	Ⓑ	4	Ⓓ
5	Ⓑ	6	Ⓐ	7	Ⓐ	8	Ⓓ
9	Ⓑ, Ⓓ	10	Ⓑ	11	Ⓐ		

PART 2

1	Ⓒ	2	Ⓑ, Ⓒ	3	Ⓒ	4	Ⓒ
5	Ⓐ	6	Ⓒ	7	Ⓐ	8	Ⓓ
9	Latitude: ③, ④ Longitude: ①, ②					10	Ⓑ
11	Ⓑ	12	Ⓒ	13	Ⓒ	14	Ⓐ
15	Proton: ③ Neutron: ① Electron: ②, ④						
16	Ⓑ	17	Ⓑ				

Scripts & Explanations

PART 1 Conversation 🎧 01-01   p.011

M Professor: Tina, I'm so glad that you dropped by. I want to speak with you for a few minutes about your paper that you turned in last week.

W Student: Oh, sure. Is there something the matter with it?

M: Uh, actually, yes, there is. I think that you must have read the directions wrong or something because you turned in a report on a topic that we won't even go over until next month.

W: Oh, my goodness! Surely you can't be serious?

M: I would never joke about something like this. Your astronomy report looked at the effects of a lunar eclipse on the Earth. However, if you would kindly take a look at this syllabus here, you'll notice that we don't even cover eclipses until next month. To be frank, I'm not sure where exactly you got the idea for this paper.

W: You know, when I was writing it, I had the feeling that there was something strange going on. I haven't missed a class all semester long, so I knew that we hadn't studied eclipses yet.

M: So how did you come to write about them in your report?

W: Well . . . It's actually a little embarrassing, but I suppose that I should tell you. You see, I lost my syllabus on the first day of class, and I was too, uh, you know, shy to ask you for another one. ⁴ So I've been relying upon one of my friends to tell me what our assignments are. He must have, uh, played a joke on me or something.

M: Not much of a friend, is he? **I think that you might need to reconsider that friendship of yours.** Anyway, it seems that although you are technically at fault, I shouldn't penalize you because another student opted to tell a lie to you. For that reason, I'm not going to give you a zero on this paper.

W: Oh, thank you so much, sir.

M: I am also going to give you another chance to rewrite this report. Now, the topic that you should have written your paper on is the moons of Saturn and how some of the major ones vary quite dramatically from one another.

W: ⁵ Wow. That really is different from what I wrote about. You must have been extremely shocked when you started reading through my paper.

M: **That's the understatement of the year.** Anyway, I shall give you four days to submit this report. Today is Thursday, so I want this report on my desk no later than noon next Monday. Do you think that you can handle it?

W: Oh, yes, sir. I'm positive I can do that report now that I know exactly what the topic is. I'm so pleased that you're giving me a second chance. A lot of professors wouldn't do that.

M: Well, I try to concern myself with what is best for my class, not others. Oh, Tina . . . One more thing.

W: Yes, sir?

M: Don't ask your friend for any more advice. I don't want you writing about something completely off the wall next time.

1 Gist-Content Question

Ⓑ When discussing the student's paper, the professor says, "I think that you must have read the directions wrong or something because you turned in a report on a topic that we won't even go over until next month."

2 Detail Question

Ⓐ The professor tells the student, "Now, the topic that you should have written your paper on is the moons of Saturn and how some of the major ones vary quite dramatically from one another."

3 Making Inferences Question

Ⓑ At the end of the conversation, the professor gives the student some advice she did not ask for. So it can be inferred that he likes to give unsolicited advice to students.

4 **Understanding Function Question**

　Ⓓ　In stating, "I think that you might need to reconsider that friendship of yours," the professor is advising the student not to be friends with the other person in her class.

5 **Understanding Attitude Question**

　Ⓑ　When remarking, "That's the understatement of the year," the professor means that the student's remark is not very strong.

PART 1 Lecture 🎧 01-02　　　　　　　　　　p.014

M Professor: The question often asked is why the United States did not enter World War II until 1941 and why it waited until after it had been attacked by Japan. To find the answer, we've got to go all the way back to World War I and then go even farther back to George Washington. Our first president advised the nation to avoid foreign entanglements, and for our first century, we were quite adept at doing so. It was not until the Spanish-American War at the end of the nineteenth century that the country's interests were carried abroad by force of arms. The Spanish-American War turned the U.S. into an imperial power with the acquisition of the Philippines, Cuba, and other Spanish territories.

　The first years of World War I were boom years for American industry as the country supplied massive amounts of materiel for the warring nations. Most went to the Allied side since our hearts were really with them. Many Americans went to Canada or England to join their armies and to look for adventure, but American armed forces stayed home. But the war wouldn't let us stay out for long. German submarines began sinking ships, ships carrying Americans and American cargo. Despite protests by the government, the sinkings continued. The Germans knew they were provoking us to go to war, but our army was small and far away and would have to cross a massive ocean full of their submarines to reach the battlefields of Europe. Well, we did declare war on April 6, 1917, rapidly expanded our military, and rushed our men to Europe, losing very few to those German subs. Many historians agree that the U.S. tipped the balance in favor of the Allies and ensured victory in 1918.

　Then came the backlash in the 1920s. Many said that the U.S. had been tricked into the war by the British and French. American industrialists earned massive profits from the blood of American men dying in Europe, said more. The theme of the greedy war profiteer took root and was hard to shake. A whole movement grew, known as isolationism, which called for the U.S. to remain out of world affairs unless threatened directly. The military was restricted by a miniscule budget. The U.S. failed to ratify the Treaty of Versailles, the treaty Germany was forced to sign in 1919 to end the war, and the U.S. refused to join the League of Nations.

　[10] These were great blows to the structure of world peace. It was obvious to all that the U.S. had been the decisive factor in defeating the Central Powers in World War I. Without the support of the United States, the League of Nations lacked the power to enforce peace. **One may look at the United Nations today and say the same thing, even with American support.** But it was this lack of support in the series of crises leading up to the outbreak of war in Europe in 1939 that had the most profound influence. Hitler provoked a series of crises with the British and French, with both nations backing down time and again as they were fearful of another war without American help.

　As this was happening in the late 1930s, the United States passed a series of laws known as the Neutrality Acts. These forbade the country from selling weapons to nations at war and stated that all strategic materiel, such as oil or steel, had to be paid for in cash and shipped on the purchasing nations' own ships. In addition, no American citizen could book passage on a ship of a nation at war, and the U.S. would not lend money to any warring nations. This last one was in response to the lack of repayment for the many loans the U.S. had given in World War I.

　When war did break out in 1939, President Roosevelt wanted to help the British and French, but his hands were tied by the isolationist movement and Neutrality Acts. In order to get around them, he enacted Lend-Lease, which allowed the U.S. to lend military supplies to the Allies with payment to be made in the future. Lend-Lease barely passed the debate in Congress. The next step was to begin a peacetime military draft, basically forcing men to do military service, an unprecedented action in American history. It too barely passed into law in 1940. [11] Roosevelt wanted to join the war against Germany, but it was impossible. When the Japanese attacked Pearl Harbor in December 1941, there were calls for a war against Japan only. **Fortunately for the world, Hitler stupidly declared war on the United States, supposedly because of Germany's treaty with Japan. In fact, he did Roosevelt a big favor.** When British Prime Minister Winston Churchill heard that the U.S. was in the war, he slept soundly for the first time during the war. He later wrote that he knew then that the Allies would win the war.

6 **Gist-Content Question**

　Ⓐ　The professor mainly discusses the historical reasons why the United States started out as neutral when World War II began.

7 Understanding Organization Question

Ⓐ At the start of the lecture, the professor remarks, "The question often asked is why the United States did not enter World War II until 1941 and why it waited until after it had been attacked by Japan. To find the answer, we've got to go all the way back to World War I and then go even farther back to George Washington." He therefore asks a question and then answers it.

8 Detail Question

Ⓓ The professor states, "German submarines began sinking ships, ships carrying Americans and American cargo. Despite protests by the government, the sinkings continued. The Germans knew they were provoking us to go to war, but our army was small and far away and would have to cross a massive ocean full of their submarines to reach the battlefields of Europe. Well, we did declare war on April 6, 1917."

9 Detail Question

Ⓑ, Ⓓ The professor states, "In addition, no American citizen could book passage on a ship of a nation at war, and the U.S. would not lend money to any warring nations."

10 Understanding Attitude Question

Ⓑ In stating, "These were great blows to the structure of world peace. It was obvious to all that the U.S. had been the decisive factor in defeating the Central Powers in World War I. Without the support of the United States, the League of Nations lacked the power to enforce peace. One may look at the United Nations today and say the same thing, even with American support," the professor means that the United Nations is unable to enforce peace, even with American help.

11 Understanding Function Question

Ⓐ The professor remarks, "Roosevelt wanted to join the war against Germany, but it was impossible. When the Japanese attacked Pearl Harbor in December 1941, there were calls for a war against Japan only. Fortunately for the world, Hitler stupidly declared war on the United States, supposedly because of Germany's treaty with Japan. In fact, he did Roosevelt a big favor." In stating that, he implies that it might have been hard for Roosevelt to declare war on Germany.

PART 2 Conversation 🎧 01-03   p.017

W Student: Excuse me, but is this the financial affairs office? There's no sign on the door, but I think I've got the right place.

M Financial Affairs Office Employee: Yes, you're correct. Sorry about having no sign. It should be back up this afternoon. Anyway, what can I do for you this morning?

W: I'm a sophomore here, and I really love everything about this university, but I'm afraid that with the new ten-percent increase in tuition, it's going to be very difficult for me to continue studying here. So, uh, I guess I'd like to know what kind of financial options are available to me.

M: All right. You've definitely come to the right place. I have no doubt at all that I'll be able to help you out. First, though, I need to ask you a few questions. To begin with, what kind of financial aid, if any, are you currently receiving?

W: Okay. Let me think about that for a second . . . First, I've got a two-thousand-dollar need-based scholarship. I've also got a student loan for the same amount. I've had one of those every semester since I've been here. I'm also receiving money through the work-study program. But that's only a few hundred dollars. So my family and I have to pay the rest of my tuition ourselves, which isn't the easiest thing in the world for us.

M: Really? Why is that? Can you give me a bit of information about your family's finances?

W: Sure. My dad is a school teacher, and my mom stays home to help raise my brothers and sister. I have three brothers and a sister, so you can imagine that my father's salary—he's a high school science teacher—doesn't go very far.

M: Yes, I think I see your point. Hmm . . . [5] Well, it's possible that you could get another need-based scholarship this year. I don't see why the school wouldn't increase the amount of money they're giving you.

W: That would be wonderful, but it's rather arbitrary, isn't it?

M: Well, yes, you're right about that. The financial aid officers try to be as fair as possible, but there are times when deserving students slip through the cracks.

W: Exactly. So my question is . . . Are there any other forms of financial aid I could, uh, I don't know, apply for, I guess, that would provide me with the extra help that I need to continue studying here?

M: The school provides athletic scholarships. You don't happen to play any sports, do you?

W: Sorry. I can't stand them. The library's my home.

M: Okay. Then we also offer a number of academic-based scholarships. You could apply for a couple of those. How are your grades?

W: My grades? Oh, I have a 3.8 GPA. It's a perfect 4.0 in my major. You know, I never even thought of academic scholarships. Are they easy to apply for?

M: Oh, yeah. There is a general form that you fill out, and then you'll automatically apply for all of the scholarships for which you qualify. Aren't computers amazing sometimes?

W: Great. So how do I get started?

M: Fill out this form and turn it back in to me.

1 Gist-Purpose Question

Ⓒ The student tells the man, "I'm afraid that with the new ten-percent increase in tuition, it's going to be very difficult for me to continue studying here. So, uh, I guess I'd like to know what kind of financial options are available to me."

2 Detail Question

Ⓑ, Ⓒ The student says, "First, I've got a two-thousand-dollar need-based scholarship. I've also got a student loan for the same amount."

3 Making Inferences Question

Ⓒ When the student says, "The library's my home," she implies that she prefers to spend her time studying.

4 Making Inferences Question

Ⓒ At the end of the conversation, the man says, "Fill out this form and turn it back in to me," so the student will probably apply for some academic scholarships.

5 Understanding Function Question

Ⓐ In stating, "That would be wonderful, but it's rather arbitrary, isn't it?" the student is expressing doubt that the idea the man proposed will succeed.

PART 2 Lecture #1 🎧 01-04   p.020

W Professor: As most of you may know, we've created a, um, a series of imaginary lines in places around the Earth for the purposes of navigation and accuracy of time. The most obvious line is the equator, which divides the Earth into its, uh, northern and southern hemispheres. The equator is a line of latitude. The lines of latitude and the lines of longitude form a grid over the surface of the Earth and allow us to navigate successfully from place to place. We can also use them to know where on the Earth a place is, even this classroom. **10 We use the circle as the reference for these lines, based on three hundred and sixty degrees. Each degree is divided further into sixty minutes and each minute into sixty seconds. Now remember not to confuse this with time. It isn't time.** Since one degree of latitude or longitude can represent many miles on the surface of the Earth, it's necessary to use minutes and seconds to narrow the range of navigation accurately to pinpoint a location.

Latitude lines start at zero degrees at the equator and then run north to the North Pole, which is ninety degrees north latitude. They also go south to the South Pole, which is ninety degrees south latitude. So we have two kinds of latitude lines, north latitude and south latitude. Latitude has been used for a long time—hundreds of years—even before Columbus reached the Americas. Sailors could judge latitude with ease based on the position of the sun above the horizon. Observations over many years gave navigators, uh, accurate charts that could tell at what angle the sun would be on a certain day of the year at a certain latitude.

Longitude was more difficult to judge. Lines of longitude run from the North to South poles. The Prime Meridian, or zero degrees, runs through Greenwich, England, which is close to London. Then we have lines of longitude running to the west of London for one hundred eighty degrees and to the east of London for one hundred eighty degrees. The two sets meet in the Pacific Ocean at what is called the International Date Line. The International Date Line is both one hundred eighty degrees west and east. This line distinguishes between when one day begins and another ends and is used for time purposes as well as navigation. Since the Earth revolves on its axis from west to east, the sunrise of a new day begins in the Pacific Ocean near Guam and then moves west to Japan, Korea, China, and farther westward across the world. It may be Tuesday morning in Tokyo, but it's Monday evening in New York.

Now, for centuries, longitude was almost, uh, impossible to judge. The only way to do so was with an accurate timepiece set for the time one left port. Unfortunately, until the eighteenth century, there were no accurate timepieces. **11 On a voyage, say, from England to Jamaica, a timepiece could be off by as much as two hours. This was caused by the imperfections of the mechanical clock in an age without batteries.** The metal parts in the clock would expand and shrink depending on the temperature and the air pressure and were also influenced by a ship's motion. Not until a clock was developed that was immune to these variables were ocean navigators able more accurately to judge longitude. I'll bet you didn't know that, did you? Nowadays, of course, we have the GPS system, and almost anybody can know where he is with a simple handheld device.

There are two other imaginary lines I want to talk about. They are not as well known as the equator or latitude or longitude. The first is the Tropic of Cancer, located at twenty-three degrees thirty minutes north latitude. Here on this map, you can see it passes through northern Mexico and North Africa. On the first day of the summer in the Northern Hemisphere, usually June twentieth or twenty-first, the sun shines directly overhead at the Tropic of Cancer. This is called the summer solstice. In the Southern Hemisphere, we have the Tropic of Capricorn at twenty-three degrees thirty minutes south latitude. Again, you can see it here on our map passing through southern Brazil and South Africa. On December twentieth or twenty-first, the sun shines directly on the Tropic of Capricorn, marking the summer solstice in the Southern Hemisphere. The zone between the two lines is called the tropical zone, and all of the world's tropical regions fall into this zone. Those to the north and south of the zone are the temperate zones.

Finally, we have the Arctic Circle at sixty-six degrees thirty minutes north latitude and the Antarctic Circle at sixty-six degrees thirty minutes south latitude. These lines mark what are called the north and southern frigid zones, where the temperatures are extremely cold and the land is almost permanently frozen.

6 Gist-Content Question

Ⓒ The professor spends the entire lecture talking about lines of latitude and longitude and how they are used.

7 Detail Question

Ⓐ The professor remarks, "The lines of latitude and the lines of longitude form a grid over the surface of the Earth, which allows us to navigate successfully from place to place. We can also use them to know where on the Earth a place is, even this classroom."

8 Understanding Organization Question

Ⓓ The professor goes into great detail about lines of latitude and longitude in the lecture.

9 Connecting Content Question

Latitude: ③, ④   Longitude: ①, ②

About latitude, the professor says, "Latitude lines start at zero degrees at the equator," and then adds, "Sailors could judge latitude with ease based on the position of the sun above the horizon." Regarding longitude, the professor remarks, "The International Date Line is both one hundred eighty degrees west and east," and also states, "Now, for centuries, longitude was almost, uh, impossible to judge."

10 Understanding Function Question

Ⓑ In stating, "Now remember not to confuse this with time. It isn't time," the professor means that the students should not confuse time and navigation despite them using the same terms.

11 Understanding Function Question

Ⓑ In stating, "On a voyage, say, from England to Jamaica, a timepiece could be off by as much as two hours. This was caused by the imperfections of the mechanical clock in an age without batteries," the professor implies that clocks in the past utilized springs.

PART 2 Lecture #2 🎧 01-05   p.023

M Professor: [17] Since this our first class, I thought we'd review what you may or may not have learned in high school chemistry. **So some of this will be old stuff for most of you . . . I hope.** Anyway, we'll begin with the basic building block of all matter, the atom and its components. The word atom comes from the Greeks and means "indivisible" because the Greeks thought that all matter was made of small components that couldn't be divided into smaller parts. Of course, we now know that isn't exactly true. The early twentieth century saw advances in our understanding of atoms with the discovery of their component parts: the neutron, the proton, and the electron. Most of the mass of an atom is made up of the nucleus, which contains the neutrons and protons. Electrons, however, orbit the nucleus. The proton has a positive charge, and the electron has a negative charge. The neutron is neutral, meaning that it has no charge.

The number of protons of an atom gives us, uh, its atomic number. This number always stays the same. Some elements have different isotopes, or types, of the same element. For example, carbon can have isotopes such as carbon-12, carbon-13, and carbon-14. Isotopes reflect, uh, the different number of neutrons in the atom. Chemical bonding can occur between elements when electrons are shared. This, of course, makes molecules, things like water, which consists of one oxygen and two hydrogen atoms.

Of the more than one hundred elements we know of today, only twelve were known to man before 1700. This included such basic metals as gold, silver, and iron. Oxygen, for example, which we all breathe every second, wasn't discovered until the 1770s. Amazing, huh? By the middle of the nineteenth century, there were dozens of known elements, and scientists were trying to find a way to organize them according to their similarities. The result is the periodic table of the elements that you see here on the board. First, I'll explain the table. Then, I'll tell you a bit of the history of its development.

Presently, there are 118 known elements, and scientists believe we'll, uh, discover more. Each block and symbol represent an element. The table is divided into columns, called groups, and rows, called periods. Let's look at hydrogen here in the top left corner, the first group of the first period. Hydrogen has only one proton, so its atomic number is one. So you can see the number one in the top right-hand corner of the hydrogen block. The elements are organized from left to right in the row, or periods, in increasing atomic numbers. The columns are based on the similar physical properties the elements have. For example, on the far left are the light metals while in the middle are the heavier metals. On the extreme right in group eighteen are what are called the noble or inert gases. These gases include helium, neon, and argon and are called inert because they bond with other elements only with extreme difficulty.

Most of the elements you see, up to element 94, are naturally occurring on the Earth. The remaining ones have been created by man, mostly in atomic reactors and particle accelerators. Now, uh, you'll see this big gap here between elements 56 and 72 in the seventh period. These are shown below and are called the rare earth elements. Below them is another gap between elements 88 and 104, which represents the radioactive earth elements, also shown below.

The history of the periodic table is one of, well, ironically, of experimentation. Different systems were tried over the years. A German chemist noticed that certain elements could be placed in groups of three with one of their atomic weights exactly between the atomic weights of the other two. This so-called Law of Triads led other scientists to examine the elements for organization. The big breakthrough came in 1869 with the work of Russian chemist Dmitri Mendeleev. Let me spell that for you on the board. It's M-E-N-D-E-L-E-E-V, Mendeleev. He wrote all the information for each known element on a separate card and then moved them around until what he had started to make some sense, uh, chemically wise that is. Thanks to his work, he is considered the creator of the modern periodic table. He also believed that a number of elements had not yet been discovered and left gaps in the table for them to be added later. One problem with Mendeleev's table was that it organized elements by atomic weight. With the discovery of the proton, a further revision by Henry Mosley, an English scientist, was made to the table in 1914. He determined that the table was best organized by atomic number based on the number of protons. Additions were later made for the rare and radioactive earth elements. Right now, scientists are trying to create new elements.

12 Gist-Content Question

Ⓒ The professor spends the entire lecture talking about the periodic table of the elements.

13 Detail Question

Ⓒ The professor remarks, "Some elements have different isotopes, or types, of the same element. For example, carbon can have isotopes such as carbon-12, carbon-13, and carbon-14. Isotopes reflect, uh, the different number of neutrons in the atom."

14 Understanding Organization Question

Ⓐ The professor divides the lecture into two main parts by first discussing the atom and then talking about the periodic table of the elements.

15 Connecting Content Question

Proton: ③   Neutron: ①   Electron: ②, ④

According to the professor, "The number of protons of an atom gives us, uh, its atomic number." About the neutron, he states, "The neutron is neutral, meaning that it has no charge. As for the electron, he remarks, "Chemical bonding can occur between elements when electrons are shared," and adds, "Most of the mass of an atom is made up of the nucleus, which contains the neutrons and protons. Electrons, however, orbit the nucleus."

16 Making Inferences Question

Ⓑ The professor comments, "Right now, scientists are trying to create new elements," which implies that the periodic table of the elements will increase in size in the future.

17 Understanding Function Question

Ⓑ In stating, "So some of this will be old stuff for most of you . . . I hope," the professor implies that most of the students should have already learned the material he will discuss.

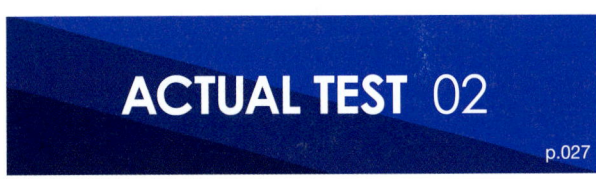

ACTUAL TEST 02
p.027

Answers

PART 1

| 1 Ⓑ | 2 Ⓒ | 3 Ⓐ | 4 Ⓐ |
| 5 Ⓓ | 6 Ⓑ | 7 Ⓓ | 8 Ⓒ |

9 Astigmatism: ③   Myopia: ②, ④   Hyperopia: ①

| 10 Ⓒ | 11 Ⓐ | | |

PART 2

1 Ⓐ	2 Ⓒ	3 Ⓐ	4 Ⓑ, Ⓓ
5 Ⓓ	6 Ⓑ	7 Ⓒ	8 Ⓓ
9 Ⓐ	10 Ⓐ	11 Ⓒ	12 Ⓒ
13 Ⓐ	14 Ⓑ	15 Ⓐ	

16 Central Asia: ①, ② North America: ③, ④
17 Ⓐ

Scripts & Explanations

PART 1 Conversation 🎧 02-01   p.029

W Student: Professor Martin, could I have a word with you for a moment, please?

M Professor: Of course. It's Janet, isn't it?

W: Wow, I can't believe you actually know my name. Our class is pretty big.

M: Well, I pride myself on being able to remember who each of my students is. I feel that doing so makes me, well, a better teacher. And I bet you're here because of your recent midterm grade, aren't you?

W: [5] Uh, yes, sir, I am. It's just that, well, you know, I've never actually gotten a C on an exam before, so I was kind of, ah, wondering what exactly I did wrong on the test. **Do you think you could give me a couple of pointers or something?**

M: Well, if I recall correctly, you're a freshman, right? And I'm willing to bet that this is one of the first tests that you've ever taken in college. Am I correct about this?

W: Yes, sir. Well, I did attend a summer program at a college between my junior and senior years in high school, but, yes, this is actually the second . . . no, the third test that I've taken in my college career.

M: All right. Well, let me explain a few things to you. First, remember that college is a lot different than high school. My history class is probably much different from the history classes you took in high school. In my class, I don't want you just to regurgitate names, dates, and places. Instead, I want you to interpret these events for me. Tell me not only what happened but why it happened. That might take a little getting used to, but it's something that you'll have to do if you want to pull out a decent grade in my course.

W: Yes, sir. I think that I understand. Do you have any other tips for me?

M: Well, I think that it might be a good idea if you were to speak with one of the department's teaching assistants. I actually have one in our class. His name is Tom, Tom Watkins. His job is to help students like you. He's really good and wants to become a teacher himself, so he should be able to, shall we say, lead you by the hand to get to where you want to be in this class.

W: Well, that sounds very helpful. Where can I find Tom's office?

M: Well, TAs don't have offices of their own, but if you go to the graduate student lounge on the third floor, you should be able to ask around and find him. He's typically at school all day long.

W: Great. I think that I'll do that.

M: Do you have anything else to talk about?

W: I know that I didn't get the best grade on the midterm, but, uh, is there a way that I can pull out an A in the class?

M: Hmm . . . I tell you what. You work hard with Tom, write an excellent report for me on our next assignment, and then ace the final, and I don't see why I shouldn't be able to reward you with a stellar grade.

1 Gist-Purpose Question

Ⓑ The student visits the professor in order to talk about the grade she received on a test.

2 Understanding Attitude Question

Ⓒ The professor shows he is interested in the student's progress by providing her with study tips and by explaining how to do well in his class.

3 Making Inferences Question

Ⓐ The professor says, "His name is Tom, Tom Watkins. His job is to help students like you. He's really good and wants to become a teacher himself, so he should be able to, shall we say, lead you by the hand to get to where you want to be in this class." He therefore implies that Tom Watkins can help the student's grade improve.

4 Making Inferences Question

Ⓐ The student will probably go to the third floor, which is where the graduate student lounge is, to find Tom Watkins.

5 Understanding Function Question

Ⓓ When the student asks the professor for some pointers, she is requesting some tips on how to study properly.

PART 1 Lecture 🎧 02-02   p.032

W Professor: When it comes to our vision, of course, all of the components of the eye are important. By the same token, some are a bit more important than others. In addition, if one of these parts becomes injured through trauma or doesn't develop correctly, problems with our vision will occur. Is everyone with me? Excellent. Can everyone see me okay? Sorry. Sorry. Poor joke. I know. Back to the eye. Can everyone please take a look at the diagram in their books on page, uh, let me see, page eighty-nine . . . ? Everyone there . . . ? Okay.

Now, as we look at this bisection of the human eye, I want you to, um, focus on the five parts, called the cornea, the iris, the pupil, the lens, and, lastly, the retina. Now, I know most of you know what the basic functions of these are, but I want to go over them briefly just to refresh everyone's memory. It will help us understand in a minute the main point of our discussion today: common eye problems and their causes. Let's work from left to right with the diagram, that is, from the external to the internal area. The first component we come across is the cornea. Who can explain its function in basic terms . . . ? Yes, over here in the front.

M Student: Professor Jacobs, the cornea is the transparent, protective shell that covers the pupil and the iris.

W: That's right. It protects the internal workings of the eye from things like foreign debris. Which brings us to the iris and the pupil, which work together in a way. The iris is the colored part of the eye that's made up of tiny muscles that control the opening and closing of the pupil, which is basically the aperture of the eye, uh, similar to that of a camera. The pupil regulates the amount of light allowed into the eye. Are you guys still able to follow everything okay . . . ? Good. What's next?

M: That would be the lens, Professor Jacobs. It focuses the image before it moves inwardly onto the retina.

W: [11] Good. And to finish up, the innermost posterior part of the eye where the final perfected, or not so perfected, as we will soon find out, image is projected and sent to the brain. **That's the barebones version of how we are able to see things, class.** Now, on to the meat of our lecture.

There are numerous problems that can occur when it comes to vision, and many of them are hereditary. The first one I'd like to discuss with you guys today is called astigmatism. Astigmatism is the most common of all other vision problems, and it stems from the cornea. When the cornea is not shaped correctly— that is, instead of being oval, it is shaped more like an egg—astigmatism is the result. Let me explain. As light enters the eye, it bends differently because of the egg-like shape of the cornea. Once this occurs, the lens has difficulty focusing on one single point because light rays are bending and creating different focal points. Because of these multi-focus points, the image becomes blurred or out of focus when it hits the retina. Is this clear to everyone . . . ? Good. Symptoms of astigmatism are, of course, blurred vision and, in more extreme cases, headaches. Are there any questions at this point, class . . . ? No. Very well.

The second vision problem I'd like to discuss is myopia. It's sometimes called nearsightedness, but don't let the name fool you. People with myopia have difficulty seeing objects far away but can see things up close very easily. This includes things such as a book or magazine or perhaps a computer screen. The cause of myopia is again a physiological one as it is with astigmatism. The actual eyeball of someone with myopia is oblong, so it's elongated lengthwise from the front to the rear. This causes the light to focus prematurely before it has a chance to reach the retina. In addition, myopia can be a degenerative condition with age. This condition is called myopic creep.

Okay, if there aren't any questions or comments, I'll start on the third common vision problem. This is called hyperopia, or farsightedness, the exact opposite, as you can imagine, of myopia. In this case, a person can see distant objects fairly easily but not ones at close distances. Again, as with myopia, the problem comes from the shape of the eyeball. With hyperopia, it is shorter than normal, it is narrower than it should be, and the light beams focus beyond, yes, beyond, the retina, causing blurred vision and difficulty seeing things up close. Unlike myopia, hyperopia sometimes does correct itself in the case of children. As they grow and develop, sometimes the shape of the eye does as well, thereby alleviating the hyperopia.

6   Gist-Content Question

Ⓑ   The professor tells the class, "It will help us understand in a minute the main point of our discussion today: common eye problems and their causes."

7   Detail Question

Ⓓ   The professor says, "The iris is the colored part of the eye that's made up of tiny muscles that control the opening and closing of the pupil, which is basically the aperture of the eye, uh, similar to that of a camera. The pupil regulates the amount of light allowed into the eye."

8   Detail Question

Ⓒ   The professor tells the class, "Once this occurs, the lens has difficulty focusing on one single point because light rays are bending and creating different focal points. Because of these multi-focus points, the image becomes blurred or out of focus when it hits the retina."

9   Connecting Content Question

Astigmatism: ③   Myopia: ②, ④   Hyperopia: ①
About astigmatism, the professor says, "When the cornea is not shaped correctly—that is, instead of being oval, it is shaped more like an egg—astigmatism is the result." Regarding myopia, the professor notes, "People with myopia have difficulty seeing objects far away but can see things up close very easily," and adds, "The actual

eyeball of someone with myopia is oblong, so it's elongated lengthwise from the front to the rear. This causes the light to focus prematurely before it has a chance to reach the retina." As for hyperopia, the professor comments, "This is called hyperopia, or farsightedness."

10 Making Inferences Question

Ⓒ The professor states, "In addition, myopia can be a degenerative condition with age. This condition is called myopic creep."

11 Understanding Function Question

Ⓐ In mentioning that she is giving "the barebones version," the professor implies that vision is more complex than the manner in which she is explaining it.

PART 2 Conversation 🎧 02-03   p.035

M Student: Excuse me, but is your name Lisa Evans? Professor Kennedy said that I should speak with you before I conduct a lab.

W Technician: Yes, I'm Lisa. First time in the lab?

M: Uh, yeah. That's right. I'm not really sure what I'm supposed to do. I wouldn't want to, uh, blow up the lab or something.

W: Yeah, making things explode can really ruin your day. Let me go over some of the safety rules in the lab so that you can become acquainted with how to act properly while you're here. This will ensure that you don't do any harm to yourself or your lab partner . . . or me, for that matter.

M: Uh, right. Okay, what do I need to know?

W: First of all, this laboratory is a serious place. We handle lots of volatile chemicals in here, so you must treat this place with respect at all times. This means you will not joke around, nor will you run, fight, or play games while you're in here.

M: ⁵Sure thing. I just want to do my lab experiment and get out of here. I won't touch anything I'm not supposed to.

W: That's a good point. First, be careful with what you touch. **If you ingest some of these chemicals, you may wake up in the emergency room.**

M: Ouch!

W: Exactly. Now, you need to wear proper clothes in the lab at all times. This means you must wear a lab coat. You can find them over there. You must also wear gloves. The gloves are by the door, so just grab a pair on the way in to the lab. You also need to wear safety goggles. Those are also by the door. As soon as you enter the lab, you need to don your gear. Don't do anything else before that.

M: Okay, but what if I have to run to the bathroom or get a drink or something?

W: Good question. When that happens, you need to remove all of your protective clothing and put it into the cleaning hamper over there. Remember that chemicals may get onto your protective clothes — that's why you wear them after all — so you shouldn't leave the lab while you're wearing them. What would happen if you got some chemicals on someone else?

M: Yeah, that wouldn't make me too popular around campus, would it?

W: Not at all.

M: Wait a second. If I have to remove all my protective gear and put it in that hamper, what do I do when I come back in? Just put on a set of entirely new stuff?

W: Bingo. You catch on pretty quickly.

M: Wow. I guess that you are pretty serious about keeping the lab safe. Has, like, anyone ever gotten hurt when they were in the lab?

W: Incidents happen every now and then, but you don't need to worry about that.

M: Hmm . . . That doesn't sound too promising.

W: Look . . . As long as you follow the safety procedures, you'll be fine. And that's what I'm here for. Now, let me continue and give you the lowdown on the rest of our rules here.

1 Gist-Content Question

Ⓐ The speakers mostly discuss safety in the laboratory.

2 Gist-Purpose Question

Ⓒ The student tells the woman that he is there to conduct an experiment.

3 Detail Question

Ⓐ The woman emphasizes that the student could harm himself with the chemicals in the lab, so she tells him that he must always wear protective gear in the laboratory.

4 Detail Question

Ⓑ, Ⓓ The woman says, "This means you must wear a lab coat. You can find them over there. You must also wear gloves."

5 Understanding Function Question

Ⓓ In stating, "If you ingest some of these chemicals, you may wake up in the emergency room," the woman implies that the student could die if he eats any of the chemicals.

PART 2 Lecture #1 🎧 02-04 p.038

M Professor: It is obvious that in mainstream America today, as well as in many other parts of the world, that forms of music such as hip-hop or rap are becoming more and more popular with young people and older people alike. The record industry, quite naturally, is reaping the rewards. What I'd like to do is take a step back right now from these styles and trace their roots. Let's find out where they came from and where they started. You may not think it is possible, but it is. Any ideas?

W Student: Didn't they, uh, evolve from blues and jazz?

M: Well, you're getting close. Yes, you are right; they are connected, but what about their predecessors? Well, class, for the answer to that, we'll have to go way back to around the fourteenth or fifteenth century. Yes, that's right. The roots of rhythm and blues, jazz, rock, rap, hip-hop, any of these styles can be traced back to early West Africa, dating all the way back to the 1500s. Remember that most African cultures were based on what is called the oral tradition. That is, the histories of the societies, of people and happenings, were passed on through words and song, not the written page as it was in Europe. One of the most important facets, or people, in this oral tradition in West Africa is the griot. The griot is a person . . . I say is, class, because griots continue to function and are still important today, some five hundred years later. He is basically the local historian responsible for remembering and telling the stories of a tribe or society through tales or song. Of course, forms of music often accompanied the stories to instill emotion and climax in the history. Rhythm and beat eventually added to the story songs. In essence, the griot helped remind people, through the oral tradition, of every aspect of what had occurred within that society in order to keep the memories, the society, alive and connected to its past. Let me try to say this more succinctly. Griots helped preserve their culture's past and also connected the present with that past. Now, are there any questions at this point? No? Okay. [11] Now, let's think back over to America really quickly. How do you think this oral tradition was passed to North America if we consider it the root of many forms of music in America?

W: Well, Professor, unfortunately, there is only one possible answer for that . . . the slave trade.

M: That's exactly right. Sure, many West Africans were seized and taken from their homelands and shipped unwillingly to the New World as slaves. They were severed from their families, culture, homeland, heritage, their entire world. But once they arrived in America, the West Indies, or other places, they continued with their oral tradition of singing about their past and telling stories of their homelands and people. As they continued this oral tradition, they were able to fill up what was hollow, what was missing inside them, and it served to reconnect them perhaps not physically, but spiritually, with their cultures and ancestors. Does everyone see this connection . . . ? Good.

Now, songs eventually took on new meanings and purposes for the slaves. First, they were a means of educating individuals about the past as well as the present. Slaves were prohibited from reading and writing, so they relied on stories and songs to educate one another about what was occurring in the area, plans for escaping, or perhaps news from the Underground Railroad in coded form. That is, class, to the average listener, like a master, the songs sounded simple and meaningless. Yet to the slaves, they were full of important information and underlying meanings. What these early slave songs did was give slaves an important boost in confidence. They gave slaves the idea that they did have some sort of control over what they said and did.

Now, let's get more to the music connection. One of the reasons the oral tradition was so successful was that it relied heavily on rhythm and repetition, which, if you think about it, most music today and in the past does. The reason the slaves incorporated rhythm and repetition was that because they were forbidden from reading and writing, it made remembering important facts and situations much easier to do. Furthermore, the early slave songs provided them with a kind of spiritual escape from the treacherous bonds of slavery. On the surface, the slaveholders seemed to control every aspect of their slaves' lives, yet through song and the oral tradition, slaves were able to be free in a sense, which often became cathartic for them.

6 Gist-Content Question
  Ⓑ The professor mostly speaks about African oral traditions and their importance and value.

7 Detail Question
  Ⓒ The professor states, "Well, class, for the answer to that, we'll have to go way back to around the fourteenth or fifteenth century. Yes, that's right. The roots of rhythm and blues, jazz, rock, rap, hip-hop, any of these styles can be traced back to early West Africa, dating all the way back to the 1500s."

8 Detail Question
  Ⓓ The professor remarks, "Slaves were prohibited from reading and writing, so they relied on stories and songs to educate one another about what was occurring in the area, plans for escaping, or perhaps news from the Underground Railroad in coded form."

9 Understanding Organization Question

Ⓐ The professor starts in the 1500s and then moves forward in time.

10 Making Inferences Question

Ⓐ The professor describes the difficult lives of slaves while also mentioning what they did to improve their lives. It can therefore be inferred that slaves were resilient.

11 Understanding Function Question

Ⓒ It can be inferred from the student's comment and from her tone of voice that she regrets that her answer is a tragic one.

PART 2 Lecture #2 🎧 02-05   p.041

M Professor: That's an excellent question. Today, most of the evidence points to Africa, probably somewhere in present-day Ethiopia, as the site of the origin of humans. Of course, scientists, especially anthropologists, have proposed this theory for many years because Africa has been the location where the oldest human fossils have been discovered. The dispute, of course, has been that older fossils could be somewhere out there, and the Africa source cannot be completely proven. But today, many geneticists are beginning to agree as they take a look at the DNA and the genetic diversity of Africa, which they maintain could have only come about from a couple hundred thousand years of mutations. What I'd like to do today is kind of take you along the journey of the first humans as they migrated out of Africa and into other regions and continents. Any questions at this point?

W Student: Um, Professor McCloud? I'm sorry, but is Ethiopia located in central Africa?

M: Well, actually, it is more toward the central eastern side of Africa. If you look at the map on page 322, you can see exactly where it is located. Got it . . . ? Excellent. Now, to move on, the earliest human fossils so far have been discovered in Omo Kibish, Ethiopia, and have been dated to around 197,000 years ago, give or take a few thousand years. Yes, I said thousands. [17] From here, most experts agree that humans began to migrate to the central western and southern areas of Africa as well as outside the continent for the first time. **Most likely, the earliest groups kept close to the Red Sea and probably migrated into areas along the eastern coast of the Mediterranean Sea as well as into the Arabian Peninsula.** Just for the earliest humans to make it out of Africa took about a hundred thousand years or so. Talk about a long journey! That's a lot of time for genes to mutate and change, and the first humans to come out of Africa probably looked quite different than their own ancient ancestors and were probably much more developed socially. Okay. Is everyone with me so far . . . ?

We're at about 100,000 years ago somewhere on the Arabian Peninsula. At this point, early groups of humans began to migrate both east and west. Most experts agree that they stuck to the coasts of the Middle East through India and journeyed down into southern Asia, where fish and other food sources were abundant. There is early human fossil evidence from the Niah Caves on the island of Borneo in the present-day state of Sarawak, Malaysia, that they reached this area about forty thousand years ago. Interestingly, there are also a couple of spots all the way down in Australia, such as at Lake Mungo, which predate the Niah Cave fossils by about 5,000 years. The Aborigines are probably the descendants of these early nomads, who made their way through southern Asia both by boats across narrow channels and across land bridges. Now, is everyone still with me? Are there any questions so far?

W: What about artifacts? Have any of them helped experts determine the course and timeline of human migration?

M: Oh, without question. Tools and even fossilized wood from fires that early humans made can be carbon dated, and they give scientists a fairly accurate date of when they were used or made. Remember that scientists do not need to locate the actual bones of humans to be able to make an educated guess as to the date of a certain area or primitive settlement. They look for any bits of evidence from sites, and once scientists find any artifacts or remains, they examine all of it very closely and then determine the general age of these items. Of course, DNA is a relatively new science compared to carbon dating and helps scientists place groups of people at certain places at certain points in history. Anyway, that's another lecture for another time. The point is that geneticists and paleoanthropologists, in general, agree on the general migration patterns of humans from the earliest beginnings based on the evidence they have gathered and investigated. Their theories match up.

So, uh, to continue, once more people settled in areas such as central Asia, early humans began to push westward over land routes into Europe. This occurred around forty to thirty thousand years ago, and around the same time, they pushed over the Himalaya Mountains into China and into other parts of Southeast and Northeast Asia. This is also around the time when they began to reach the eastern edge of Asia and migrated north into Siberia. Many experts, but not, by any means, all of them, agree that around twenty to fifteen thousand years ago, ocean levels were low enough for humans to cross over a land bridge and enter North America for the first time.

12 Gist-Content Question

Ⓒ The professor mostly discusses the earliest movements of humans and how scientists have tracked these movements.

13 Detail Question

Ⓐ The professor states, "There is early human fossil evidence from the Niah Caves on the island of Borneo in the present-day state of Sarawak, Malaysia, that they reached this area about forty thousand years ago."

14 Detail Question

Ⓑ The professor remarks, "The point is that geneticists and paleoanthropologists, in general, agree on the general migration patterns of humans from the earliest beginnings based on the evidence they have gathered and investigated. Their theories match up."

15 Understanding Organization Question

Ⓐ The professor discusses the events in his lecture in chronological order.

16 Connecting Content Question

Central Asia: 1, 2 North America: 3, 4

About Central Asia, the professor states, "So, uh, to continue, once more people settled in areas such as central Asia, early humans began to push westward over land routes into Europe. This occurred around forty to thirty thousand years ago, and around the same time, they pushed over the Himalaya Mountains into China and into other parts of Southeast and Northeast Asia." As for North America, the professor remarks, "Many experts, but not, by any means, all of them, agree that around twenty to fifteen thousand years, ocean levels were low enough for humans to cross over a land bridge and enter North America for the first time."

17 Understanding Function Question

Ⓐ In stating, "Most likely, the earliest groups kept close to the Red Sea and probably migrated into areas along the eastern coast of the Mediterranean Sea as well as into the Arabian Peninsula," the professor implies that the sea provided food for early humans.

ACTUAL TEST 03

Answers

PART 1

1 Ⓑ	2 Ⓓ	3 Ⓒ	4 Ⓐ
5 Ⓓ	6 Ⓐ	7 Ⓐ,Ⓑ	8 Ⓑ
9 Ⓓ	10 Ⓒ	11 Ⓓ	

PART 2

| 1 Ⓑ | 2 Ⓓ | 3 Ⓒ | 4 Ⓐ |
| 5 Ⓑ | 6 Ⓒ,Ⓓ | 7 Ⓑ | 8 Ⓐ |

9 Childhood: 4 Middle Years: 1, 2 Later Life: 3

| 10 Ⓑ | 11 Ⓒ | 12 Ⓒ | 13 Ⓑ |
| 14 Ⓓ | 15 Ⓓ | 16 Ⓐ | 17 Ⓓ |

Scripts & Explanations

PART 1 Conversation 03-01

W Dean of Student Life: Good morning. Please come in and have a seat. It's a pleasure to meet you, Mr. Jackson.

M Student: Thank you, ma'am. The pleasure is all mine.

W: So you're here to talk about the living conditions in the school dormitories, uh, particularly North Hall, where you live. Is that correct?

M: It is. As you are the dean of student life, I believe you're the proper person to speak with since you should be able to help us implement some changes to improve the dorms. My assumption is correct, isn't it?

W: Well, I can't promise that I'll be able to effect any changes you suggest. It basically depends upon what you tell me. But I'm definitely the person to speak with to get the process started.

M: Wonderful.

W: So, Mr. Jackson, how about telling me what's on your mind?

M: Yes, ma'am. First, I was selected as the representative of students living in North Hall. Before I scheduled this meeting, the residents of the dorm got together to discuss the primary issues which concern us. So I would like to let you know I am speaking for all of the residents of North Hall, uh, not just myself.

W: Thank you for informing me.

M: You're welcome. Now the first point of contention is the cleanliness of the dorm. We students were under the impression that custodians would be cleaning the dorm bathrooms, hallways, and lounges every day. Uh . . . maybe not on weekends. But definitely on weekdays. Anyway, that's most assuredly not the case as cleaning crews have only been coming three times a week, and the dorms can be a bit messy at times.

W: Hmm . . . I'll have to look into that. Our contract with the company handling that matter stipulates that the areas you mentioned should be cleaned daily. If the company isn't doing that . . . Well, that's not good. Thank you for bringing that to my attention. What else do you have?

M: Many students are unhappy about what they consider excessive noise regulations.

W: In what regard?

M: Several students have received fines from resident assistants in the past two weeks. The RAs claimed the students were making too much noise after ten at night. I know one of those students. She was listening to some music, but you could barely hear it in the hallway. I think some RAs are a bit, uh, overzealous in enforcing the new noise regulations.

W: Yes, I've heard the same complaint from other students. I think I'll have to speak with some individual resident assistants to find out what's going on.

M: Excellent. Thank you.

W: Do you have anything else for me?

M: There are several minor items on the list, but I don't want to bother you with them right now. Instead, I'll just give you the list. Uh, here you are . . . ⁵ But I would like to discuss one last point.

W: Of course.

M: Many students request that cooking facilities be installed in the dorm.

W: **I'm sorry, but that's simply not feasible for your dorm.** It's old, and installing those kinds of facilities would require the complete renovation of the dorm. However, the two new dorms being constructed will have the facilities you requested.

M: I was expecting that response. But I told the students I would still ask.

1 Gist-Content Question

Ⓑ The woman says, "So you're here to talk about the living conditions in the school dormitories, uh, particularly North Hall, where you live."

2 Detail Question

Ⓓ The student states, "I was selected as the representative of students living in North Hall."

3 Understanding Organization Question

Ⓒ The woman remarks, "Our contract with the company handling that matter stipulates that the areas you mentioned should be cleaned daily. If the company isn't doing that . . . Well, that's not good."

4 Making Inferences Question

Ⓐ When the woman states, "I think I'll have to speak with some individual resident assistants to find out what's going on," it can be inferred that she will meet some residential assistants soon.

5 Understanding Function Question

Ⓓ When the woman says, "I'm sorry, but that's simply not feasible for your dorm," she is responding negatively to the student's request.

PART 1 Lecture 🎧 03-02

W Professor: So those are the major types of rivers in the world. Now, as you may be aware, many rivers form deltas at their mouths. The Mississippi River forms one of the most recognizable deltas in the world. The term "delta" was coined by the Greek historian Herodotus because the shape of the delta of the Nile River in Egypt is shaped like the Greek letter delta. The Amazon River has the largest delta in the world, and the Yellow River in China has the greatest sediment flow, which is very important in delta formation.

Sediment flow is what creates a delta. Rock is eroded by wind and water, and many of the eroded parts end up in the water system at some point and, eventually, in the great rivers of the world. As a river moves toward the ocean or a large lake, it picks up this eroded dirt and sand. When the river reaches a large body of water, the force of the river slows, and the sediment is deposited. The finer particles are carried farther from shore, and the coarser ones are heavier and fall to the seabed first. You therefore have a gentle slope underwater with the heavy buildup near the river's mouth and which gradually slopes downward the farther out to sea it goes. As the delta grows outward, different types of material form layers on top of one another. Often, at the bottom of the delta there are mud with silt on top, then fine sand, and finally, coarser sand on top. It can build up for many centuries, and if there is enough sediment, it can produce islands and cause the river to divert into many different channels.

In fact, the Mississippi has had seven recognizable delta formations in different locations over its long history with one even having the mouth of the river where present-day New Orleans is. The current form of the Mississippi delta is approximately six hundred years old. When a river overflows, the coarser sand sediment is sometimes deposited on the river banks, which forms natural levees. A levee is like a long pile of dirt. They are often found along rivers that are prone to flooding. As I said, some are natural whereas many are manmade. Flooding was one of the great dilemmas of the ancient world, especially in ancient China and Egypt. Flooding allowed rich deposits of sediment to be deposited, which enriched the soil for growing food. But flooding is also very disruptive to life and causes massive damage and loss of life at times. The Egyptians built the Aswan Dam to control the flooding of the Nile.

The formation of a river delta depends on several factors. Chief among these are the speed of the river's water flow and the nature of the body of water the mouth meets, particularly its tides and wave energy. Rivers with great flow, such as the Amazon, can carry the sediment farther and thus create larger deltas. Slower rivers deposit their sediment much sooner. In addition, the condition of the body of water will determine what type of delta there is. In the Gulf of Mexico, where the Mississippi comes out, there is a very mild body of water with weak tides and wave forces. The speed of the Mississippi's flow is greater than the tide and wave forces, so the delta forms in long fingerlike protrusions, and the delta grows far from the coast.

[11] In contrast, the Nile delta has a much smoother coastline because the Mediterranean waves force the deposited sands back into long smooth lines. Since the Egyptians built the massive dam to control the Nile, the amount of sediment has been considerably reduced. **The delta is actually receding because of the force of the waves.** The Niger River in West Africa is another such example since the Atlantic Ocean has both strong tides and waves. Other deltas do not appear to be deltas at all but are more like estuaries because the strength of the tides and the waves is so strong in those areas.

Deltas are the sites of several of the world's great oil fields, with the Niger and Mississippi rivers among the largest. These rivers have been depositing sediment for millions of years, and the sediment has settled and crushed massive amounts of plant and animal life, which has created oil and its byproducts. River deltas are also homes to diverse ecosystems with extensive marshlands, both fresh and salt water, supporting many reptilian, amphibian, and aquatic life forms. There are also large numbers of birds in these deltas. Man's intrusion into the deltas sometimes upsets this balance. The Nile delta was once a great fishing ground, but since the dam was built, the sediment, rich with nutrients, are fewer, and the fish are therefore also fewer in number.

6 Gist-Content Question

(A) The professor mostly lectures on how deltas are formed.

7 Detail Question

(A), (B) The professor states, "The formation of a river delta depends on several factors. Chief among these are the speed of the river's water flow and the nature of the body of water the mouth meets, particularly its tides and wave energy."

8 Understanding Organization Question

(B) The professor begins by pointing out a fact about deltas and then provides various examples throughout her lecture.

9 Understanding Attitude Question

(D) In stating, "Flooding was one of the great dilemmas of the ancient world, especially in ancient China and Egypt. Flooding allowed rich deposits of sediment to be deposited, which enriched the soil for growing food. But flooding is also very disruptive to life and causes massive damage and loss of life at times," the professor indicates that she believes the flooding of rivers has both positive and negative effects.

10 Making Inferences Question

(C) The professor notes, "Since the Egyptians built the massive dam to control the Nile, the amount of sediment has been considerably reduced. The delta is actually receding because of the force of the waves." In stating that, she implies that the Aswan Dam is an ecological mistake.

11 Understanding Attitude Question

(D) In stating that the delta is receding, the professor means that the Nile delta is shrinking because of the action of waves.

PART 2 Conversation 🎧 03-03   p.053

W Student: Sir, I wonder if you have some time to discuss my thesis.

M Professor: I think I can spare a few minutes. What is your subject about?

W: I was hoping you could help with that. I'm having a bit of trouble deciding on a topic. It's already October, and I need to get started if I hope to finish by next spring.

M: Well, hopefully it will be related to psychology.

W: Yes, sir, of course. What I'm really interested in are child development and autism.

M: That is an interesting field, but there are some dangers in choosing it as a major thesis topic.

W: Dangers? I don't understand what you mean.

M: Autism is a very controversial subject these days. Some believe it is a hereditary disorder, others believe it is caused by early childhood immunizations, and still others believe it is a product of early childhood rearing. I'm just afraid you will get lost in a jungle of differing opinions and lose focus on your paper.

W: Actually, I have been volunteering at the autism center on campus, so I was hoping to do a research report on the children I have been observing.

M: Well, that sounds like an excellent idea. I suggest that you focus on patterns of behavior and reactions to certain stimuli.

W: Yes, I was thinking along the same lines. What would you suggest for the number of subjects to be observed?

M: The larger the sample, the better. How many children are currently in the center?

W: I believe about ten are regular, and another five or six come once in a while.

M: Well, I would concentrate on the ones that come regularly so that you can have a greater amount of data.

W: But I really don't want to leave the others out of the study if that's possible.

M: You know, um, it might be interesting to find out why they are not attending the center regularly.

W: I've talked to some of the parents, and they just don't have the time to bring them. I also believe that there are some who have difficult family situations. At least two of the mothers are divorced, and another is a single mom.

M: That must be tough. I couldn't imagine raising an autistic child by myself. Here's a suggestion: Compare the progress of the students who attend regular sessions at the center with those who don't.

W: I think that's a great idea, but I'd have to have the permission of the parents. I don't want them to think of their child as a guinea pig.

M: No, of course not. You'll have to handle it very delicately. In addition, be sure that you don't have any prejudicial opinions. ⁵ You may feel that the children in the center will automatically do better than the children who come irregularly. But what we have found over the years is that every autistic child is different, so some do well without attending special classes while others make no progress whatsoever despite years of help. **Just keep an open mind when conducting the study.**

1 Gist-Purpose Question
Ⓑ About her thesis, the student says, "I'm having a bit of trouble deciding on a topic."

2 Detail Question
Ⓓ The professor tells the student, "Autism is a very controversial subject these days. Some believe it is a hereditary disorder, others believe it is caused by early childhood immunizations, and still others believe it is a product of early childhood rearing. I'm just afraid you will get lost in a jungle of differing opinions and lose focus on your paper."

3 Understanding Attitude Question
Ⓒ The professor expresses sympathy for the mothers by stating, "That must be tough. I couldn't imagine raising an autistic child by myself."

4 Making Inferences Question
Ⓐ It can be inferred that the professor has some knowledge on the student's preferred topic since she asks him for advice.

5 Understanding Attitude Question
Ⓑ When the professor tells the student to "keep an open mind," he means that she should not make any judgments until she completes her research.

PART 2 Lecture #1 03-04

M Professor: Most people believe that the greatest conqueror in the world was Alexander the Great, but they are wrong. In actuality, it was Genghis Khan, the great early thirteenth-century Mongol leader. With his horse-riding, arrow-shooting hordes, he conquered a territory greater than any other leader either before or after him. What makes Genghis Khan's story even more remarkable are his humble beginnings and the backwardness of the people he led. But it was on account of these factors, not in spite of them, that Genghis was able to forge his people into the greatest class of warriors the world has ever known.

Genghis Khan was born in Mongolia near the present-day border with Russia in 1162. Mongolia at that time wasn't a nation but was a land of many tribes, which were usually warring with one another. Genghis's mother was actually captured from another tribe by his father.

His real name was Temujin, and Genghis Khan means "Great Leader." His tribe was one of the poorer ones as its members lived north of the great Gobi Desert in an area with marginal resources. The people were herders of livestock and had hard lives in which they depended on their animals for much of their livelihood. Most of all, they were master horse breeders and riders. Most Mongols could ride and shoot the bow and arrow from horseback at an early age. This mobility was their greatest asset in warfare.

Genghis's father was killed when he was only nine years old, and the tribe cast his family out. Basically, they were considered a burden since the family consisted of Genghis's father's two wives and several children and had no men to protect them. Yes, Mongols then had more than one wife. Soon after his father's death, Genghis's first challenge was from his older half-brother over leadership of the family. Many accounts say that Genghis stalked and killed his older half-brother. This crime became widely known, which further set Genghis's family apart from the tribes and set him on the road to being a great warrior. By adulthood, Genghis had been through a series of rough-and-tumble encounters with various adversaries, who tried to enslave or kill him and his family. This early life made him a hardened warrior and taught him many useful strategies he would later use on the battlefield.

Genghis's next great challenge came when a neighboring tribe captured his wife. He could have relented and gotten another bride, but he decided to attack. With the help of an allied tribe, Genghis was successful. But his wife was pregnant, and a son was born. For the rest of his life, the Mongols secretly and at times openly speculated that Genghis's oldest son was not his but that the father was the man who had captured his wife. This had serious consequences for the line of succession when Genghis neared the end of his life. After the recapture of his wife, Genghis set his mind toward either conquering the other tribes in the area or allying himself with them. His reputation as a fierce warrior and master tactician grew, and over the next ten years, a fierce civil war engulfed the Mongol tribes until Genghis was master of them all.

The Mongols now eyed the rich lands south of the Gobi Desert. After conquering some cities and capturing their luxuries, the Mongols' taste for the rich life grew. **[11]** To please his people, Genghis and his army set off on further conquests. The rich lands of modern-day Pakistan, Afghanistan, and Iran beckoned. Genghis often sent an emissary ahead to a city to ask for its submission.

If the people killed his emissary or refused to surrender, the Mongols showed no mercy. But if they did give up, the Mongols were very civil conquerors. Their reputation soon preceded them, and rumors of these unstoppable warriors from the east floated all the way to Europe. Much of the Middle East and Russia as well as parts of Eastern Europe were conquered by the Mongols. Only India, with its hot, muggy, disease-ridden climate unsuitable for Mongol warriors managed to avoid becoming a vassal state.

Despite his great skills at warfare and administration, Genghis failed to provide for the longevity of his empire. He had four sons with the oldest one's parentage in dispute. Because of this, his two eldest sons hated each other intensely, so Genghis made his third son his successor. He, unfortunately, was an alcoholic and wasted the wealth Genghis had captured. Genghis was a better leader than teacher and had trouble teaching his sons things he knew by instinct from his years of strife and warfare. Genghis died in 1227. Some accounts say he died from a fall from his horse. His sons all died early, and the empire did not last long, but its legacy was far reaching as it influenced the world from China to the gates of Vienna.

6 Gist-Content Question

Ⓒ, Ⓓ The professor focuses mostly on the childhood of Genghis Khan and his rise to power.

7 Detail Question

Ⓑ The professor notes, "Genghis's first challenge was from his older half-brother over leadership of the family. Many accounts say that Genghis stalked and killed his older half-brother. This crime became widely known, which further set Genghis's family apart from the tribes and set him on the road to being a great warrior."

8 Understanding Organization Question

Ⓐ The professor stresses how Genghis Khan became a great warrior when focusing on his early life.

9 Connecting Content Question

Childhood: [4] Middle Years: [1], [2] Later Life: [3]
According to the professor, Genghis Khan killed his half-brother during his childhood. During his middle years, his wife was kidnapped, and he defeated the other Mongol tribes. In his later life, there was a succession crisis.

10 Making Inferences Question

Ⓑ The professor implies that Genghis Khan's first son was not really his, so it can be inferred that the second son believed he was the first real son of Genghis Khan.

11 Understanding Function Question

Ⓒ The professor says, "If the people killed his emissary or refused to surrender, the Mongols showed no mercy," in order to emphasize that the Mongols treated some of the people that they conquered very harshly.

PART 2 Lecture #2 🎧 03-05   p.059

W Professor: Now, I'd like to discuss the origins of blood transfusions and the types of blood humans have. You may know that nowadays, blood transfusions, or the giving of one person's blood to another, are a common practice. Some of you may even have received blood from a donor if you've had an accident or operation. However, this is a very recent phenomenon in historical terms. [16] **In fact, it may surprise you, but bloodletting, the releasing of blood from the body, was a more common treatment even into the nineteenth century.** Perhaps the most famous case was the death of President George Washington, who had repeated bloodlettings during an illness at the end of his life. Some historians and medical experts partially blame his death on that.

The first transfusion we have a record of occurred in France in 1667, where the blood of a cow was transfused into a mental patient. The patient survived, but the incident outraged the religious sensitivities of the times, and no further experiments were tried. The next absolute documentation of a blood transfusion occurred in 1818 when an English physician saved a woman who had just given birth by giving her a blood transfusion. By the twentieth century, transfusions were commonplace, and they have been responsible for saving tens of thousands of lives in the wars of the last one hundred years.

Blood is usually stored as whole blood or plasma. Blood can be separated into its various parts, and plasma is the most important. Plasma is a clear, yellowish liquid that is ninety percent water and is the part of the blood that contains a lot of protein. It is used to treat trauma victims with lots of blood loss since it has very good clotting properties, which are essential for reducing blood loss. It is also easier to store and refrigerate than whole blood. Nowadays, people are asked to donate their blood at blood banks or hospitals. Some places even pay people to provide their blood. The Red Cross is one of the biggest collectors of blood in the United States these days. However, it and many other blood banks faced a tragic scandal in the early 1980s. First hepatitis and then HIV, the virus that causes AIDS, entered the blood bank system and made their way to thousands of patients in operations and medical treatments. Some of the biggest sufferers were hemophiliacs. Approximately 8,000 hemophiliacs got HIV, and about 6,000 of them died.

Now, all blood is rigorously screened for HIV and other viruses, but the fallout from that scandal has caused many people to refuse to donate blood even now, several decades later. Some people erroneously believe that just giving blood will give them HIV. Nothing could be further from the truth. Unfortunately, because of these fears, not enough blood is now in storage even to meet existing needs. Imagine what would happen if we had a disaster. The blood system would be overwhelmed.

Now I want to talk about different blood types and why one type of blood may or may not be transfused into a patient. There are four basic blood types: A, B, AB, and O. Each blood cell has an antigen, a kind of protein, on its surface. An antigen is a substance that can introduce antibodies, which are the part of the immune system that fights disease. The letters for the blood groups represent these antigens. Another factor in typing blood is the Rhesus, or Rh, factor. It is named for the rhesus monkey, in which it was first discovered. This divides blood further into Rh positive and Rh negative blood groups. So a person could have A negative, A positive, B negative, B positive, AB negative, AB positive, O negative, or O positive blood. In the United States, approximately thirty-seven percent of people have O positive blood. Thirty-four percent have A positive, and ten percent have B positive blood. The rarest blood type is AB negative. Eighty-five percent of Americans have Rh positive blood.

[17] In a transfusion, a patient must receive a blood type that is compatible with his blood. Blood type O negative is the best for transfusions because everyone can accept it in a transfusion. **Unfortunately, only six percent of Americans have O negative blood, which is reflected in the amount donated.** A person with AB positive blood type is very lucky because he can use any blood for a transfusion. For some of the others, they can only accept their own blood type and one other that is closely related. If a patient receives the wrong blood, the antigens reject it and cause the red blood cells to start sticking together. This can cause serious problems. A clot, or lump of blood, can form. If it goes to the heart, lungs, or brain, it can cause a stroke or even death.

12 Gist-Content Question

Ⓒ The professor mostly talks about the history of blood transfusions as well as different blood types.

13 Detail Question

   Ⓑ The professor remarks, "By the twentieth century, transfusions were commonplace, and they have been responsible for saving tens of thousands of lives in the wars of the last one hundred years."

14 Understanding Attitude Question

   Ⓓ The professor notes, "Some people erroneously believe that just giving blood will give them HIV. Nothing could be further from the truth. Unfortunately, because of these fears, not enough blood is now in storage even to meet existing needs."

15 Making Inferences Question

   Ⓓ The professor says, "In the United States, approximately thirty-seven percent of people have O positive blood. Thirty–four percent have A positive, and ten percent have B positive blood. The rarest blood type is AB negative." It can therefore be inferred that fewer than ten percent of Americans have AB blood.

16 Understanding Function Question

   Ⓐ In stating, "In fact, it may surprise you, but bloodletting, the releasing of blood from the body, was a more common treatment even into the nineteenth century," the professor implies that bloodletting was an accepted medical practice in the past.

17 Understanding Function Question

   Ⓓ In stating, "Unfortunately, only six percent of Americans have O negative blood, which is reflected in the amount donated," the professor means that there is not enough O negative blood donated.

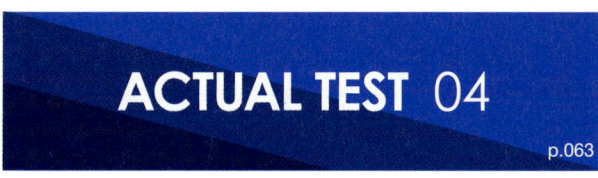

ACTUAL TEST 04

p.063

Answers

PART 1

1 Ⓑ	2 Ⓑ	3 Ⓒ	4 Ⓒ
5 Ⓓ	6 Ⓑ	7 Ⓒ, Ⓓ	8 Ⓐ
9 Ⓑ	10 Clipper Aircraft: 1, 3 Boeing 747: 2, 4		
11 Ⓑ	12 Ⓓ	13 Ⓒ	14 Ⓑ
15 Ⓑ	16 Smith: 1, 4 Frost: 2, 3		
17 Ⓐ			

PART 2

1 Ⓐ	2 Ⓒ	3 Ⓐ	4 Ⓒ
5 Ⓑ	6 Ⓒ	7 Ⓐ	8 Ⓓ
9 Ⓑ	10 Ⓐ		
11 Cardiac: 4 Smooth: 2 Skeletal: 1, 3			

Scripts & Explanations

PART 1 Conversation 🎧 04-01 p.065

M Student: Hello. Are you Miss Stevens? I was told that you're the person to speak to with regard to meal plans.

W Employee: Yes, I'm Miss Stevens. What can I help you with?

M: I'm here about my meal plan. I'm currently on a meal plan that provides me with twenty-one meals a week. You know, breakfast, lunch, and dinner. But I just don't think it's the right one for me since I almost never eat breakfast.

W: ⁵ Well, we have a meal plan that provides fourteen meals a week. If you never eat breakfast, that might be the ideal one for you.

M: Hmm . . . That may have potential. But here's another thing. I actually don't even eat lunch at the cafeteria that often. I sometimes skip it completely, or I just go to the campus center and order a pizza or something like that. It's not the healthiest of options, but that's what I do anyway.

W: Okay. We offer a couple of other meal plans. You could get the seven-a-week meal plan or the ten-a-week meal plan. If you actually have lunch in the cafeteria sometimes, I'd recommend the ten-a-week plan.

M: Yeah, I estimate that I eat at the cafeteria about that many times a week. So how much does it cost?

W: It's only $1,500 a semester, so it's $600 cheaper than the twenty-one-a-week meal plan.

M: Sweet. So I'll get to save a lot of money. Uh, will you just give me the cash, or will you credit it to my school account? I'd really love to get that money right now.

W: I bet you would. Unfortunately, we don't do cash transactions here, so I'll only be able to credit your account. But the money should be available at the Bursar's office this afternoon.

M: Great. So what do I need to do?

W: If I could see your student ID card, then I can get the paperwork started. You have your ID card with you, don't you?

M: Oh, yeah. Sure. It's right here . . . Here you are.

W: Thank you very much, Mr. . . . Carter. Okay, uh, let me just put this identification number into the computer, and . . . Uh-oh. I think that we have a small problem here.

M: A problem? What are you talking about?

W: Well, according to your card, you're a first-year student. And the computer here tells me that you currently live in one of the on-campus dormitories. Is this correct?

M: Yeah, it is. What does that have to do with me changing my meal plan?

W: The university has specific rules on students like you changing their meal plans. According to our rules, all first-year students who live on campus must have at least a fourteen-a-week meal plan. The school likes to make sure that the students all have access to at least two meals a day. So I cannot allow you to sign up for the ten-a-week meal plan. I can, however, let you downgrade to the fourteen-a-week plan.

M: I guess I don't have much of a choice then.

W: Okay. Let me get to work on making the change then.

1 Gist-Content Question

B   The speakers are mostly talking about which meal plan options are available for the student.

2 Detail Question

B   After the woman recommends the ten-a-week plan, the student says, "Yeah, I estimate that I eat at the cafeteria about that many times a week."

3 Understanding Attitude Question

C   The employee is very informative toward the student as she provides him with all of the information he needs to make his choice.

4 Making Inferences Question

C   When the employee says that the student can only downgrade to the fourteen-a-week plan, the student says that he has no choice, so he will most likely sign up for that meal plan next.

5 Understanding Function Question

D   When the student says that the woman's suggestion has potential, it can be inferred that he will consider signing up for the meal plan that she recommends.

PART 1 Lecture #1 04-02

M1 Professor: Charles Lindbergh's first transatlantic flight opened a whole new world of possibilities for aviation, especially commercial aviation. Once he was able to breach the great watery divide between North America and Europe, the sky was the limit. Pan American Airways was the first to make the dream of carrying passengers across the oceans into a reality. It implemented a fleet of planes, called Clippers, to become the first commercial planes to cross the vast oceans, which created an air network that would enable Pan Am basically to connect the far reaches of the world. This was happening in the U.S. in the 1930s, and after a couple of test runs, first across the Pacific and then the Atlantic, the Pan American Airways' plane the *Dixie Clipper* became the first transatlantic commercial flight with passengers ever on June 28, 1939.

W Student: Um, Professor, was there any special significance to the name Clipper?

M1: Excellent question. Pan Am named the plane after the swift, sleek clipper ships of the nineteenth century. Oh, that brings us to another important point about the Clipper planes. They were literally flying cruise ships. They were monsters. They were the juggernauts of the sky and by far the largest commercial planes of their day. It wasn't until the late 1960s . . . I believe it was 1969, when Boeing came out with the 747, that the Clipper was ultimately eclipsed in size by a new design. By the way, Boeing also manufactured the Clipper class of planes. Quite remarkable, isn't it? Again, they were literally flying ocean vessels, meaning that instead of landing and taking off from land, the Clippers used water as their runway.

But let me get back to the design of the Clipper. I wish I had a couple of slides of them to show you. They were far from the sardine-can-like flights we are subjected to today. Perhaps, next week I'll try to bring some in, but anyway, they were flying five-star hotels. Passengers enjoyed first-class luxury on their entire trip. On the inaugural flight of the *Dixie Clipper* across the Atlantic, twenty-two passengers enjoyed a main sitting area equipped with plush sofas and reclining areas with ample room for socializing and milling around. Separate lounges for cocktail hour also occupied the rear of the plane. The main area was converted into a dining compartment complete with linens on the tables and fine silver utensils. Pan Am made sure that the first flight service over the Atlantic left no creature comfort out by any means. Of course, the first passengers were the upper crust of society and paid almost ten thousand dollars in today's monetary equivalent, fairly equal to the cost of a flight on the now defunct Concorde but, obviously, with much more legroom.

M2 Student: Excuse me, Professor. How long did a one-way crossing take?

M1: Another excellent question. You guys must be reading my mind. A typical trip usually took about a full day. It depended on the weather. The plane would usually refuel in the Azores when bound for Europe or near Newfoundland on its return to the States. I mean, think about it. Today, we take air travel for granted in a way. We complain about long lines and escalating prices. They cause lots of headaches. But back then, flying was a privilege. It was an adventure for both the pilots and the passengers who first crossed back and forth over the Atlantic and other oceans from continent to continent. ¹¹Clearly, what Pan Am's Clipper flights did was begin to bring the world closer together. In a way, they were the earliest stage of what today has come to be called globalization in that air travel allows countries to work and develop more closely together. Geography and distances were no longer barriers for travel and cultural exchange. **They contributed to a kind of international cohesion that was beginning to emerge due to air travel across the oceans.** Yes, we owe a lot to the vision of Pan American Airways and its early Clipper aircraft. Even today, the North Atlantic commercial flights remain the most lucrative market in the world.

M2: But why haven't many of us even heard of the Clipper flights?

M1: I'm impressed, class. You're really on the ball today. That was another excellent question. Well, for one thing, World War II began, which put an immediate halt on all commercial airline service to Europe as well as to Asia. Oh, remember that Pan Am also had transpacific flights from the west coast of the U.S. to Asia at the time. These flights usually island hopped their way to Hong Kong. In addition, once the U.S. entered the war, a number of the original Clippers were reconfigured as cargo and troop transports headed for the battlefields of Europe.

6 Gist-Content Question

Ⓑ The professor mostly describes the planes that flew on transatlantic flights and talks about their impact on the future.

7 Detail Question

Ⓒ, Ⓓ The professor says, "It implemented a fleet of planes, called Clippers, to become the first commercial planes to cross the vast oceans, which created an air network that would enable Pan Am basically to connect the far reaches of the world."

8 Understanding Attitude Question

Ⓐ The professor is clearly impressed by the first-class travel the Clippers provided when he tells the class about them.

9 Understanding Attitude Question

Ⓑ The professor says, "They were far from the sardine-can-like flights we are subjected to today," and then adds, "Of course, the first passengers were the upper crust of society and paid almost ten thousand dollars in today's monetary equivalent, fairly equal to the cost of a flight on the now defunct Concorde but, obviously, with much more legroom," which both imply that modern commercial aircraft provide minimal comfort in comparison to the Clippers.

10 Connecting Content Question

Clipper Aircraft: ①, ③ Boeing 747: ②, ④

About the Clipper, the professor says, "Of course, the first passengers were the upper crust of society and paid almost ten thousand dollars in today's monetary equivalent, fairly equal to the cost of a flight on the now defunct Concorde," and then adds, "In addition, once the U.S. entered the war, a number of the original Clippers were reconfigured as cargo and troop transports headed for the battlefields of Europe." As for the Boeing 747, the professor mentions, "I believe it was 1969, when Boeing came out with the 747, that the Clipper was ultimately eclipsed in size by a new design."

11 Understanding Function Question

Ⓑ In stating, "They contributed to a kind of international cohesion that was beginning to emerge due to air travel across the ocean," the professor implies that the Clipper service by Pan Am helped start to unite the people of the world.

PART 1 Lecture #2 🎧 04-03   p.071

W Professor: Now, what I'd like to do is compare two popular modern poems by two authors, Stevie Smith and Robert Frost. Both address the theme of perception and how our perceptions are not always what they seem to be. I'd like to begin with Stevie Smith's poem entitled *Not Waving, But Drowning*, which is actually one of my personal favorites. Everyone has already read the poetry like I asked for homework, right?

M Student: I did, Professor. Um, was Mr. Smith also an American poet?

W: Well, it seems as if you failed to read the bio, Mr. Aldrich, doesn't it? Remember, class, that you should always read the short biography in the back of your text before you read the poem. What that does is give you a more specific context in which to read the poem, and it will help you understand where the poem comes from and the poet's intentions and motives.

Now, back to Mr. Aldrich's question. The answer is no. Stevie Smith was actually British. In addition, Stevie Smith is a penname, which might fool many of you when it comes to the gender of the author. Now, we might perceive the poem on one level as a tragic occurrence. An individual is swimming in the ocean. He swims too far out, gets in trouble, drowns, and his body washes up on the shore. At this point, people gather around the person and discuss between themselves what went wrong. Physically, the person is dead. Then why is the drowned individual speaking, moaning in the first and last stanzas, with the words only heard by us, the reader? Well, this is the magic of the poem and of Stevie Smith's technique. Though dead, the individual continues to plea for help and to explain how he was "much too far out all my life." His death, then, is simply a culmination of years and years of trouble, pain, and suffering. He tried to mask it by seeming happy, which is symbolized by waving in the title, yet internally, he was in great distress, symbolized by the word "drowning" in the title. Only after death is the person able to vocalize himself and ask for help, but by then it is too late. How we perceive someone or a situation can be deceiving. This, I think, is the main message of the poem, class. Personally, I don't believe the person drowned at all, which would be an accident. I don't want to be too morbid, but if the person was as troubled as he seems in the poem, the drowning was probably more on purpose than simply a freak accident.

M: Professor, you got all of that out of a little twelve-line poem?

W: ¹⁷ Sure, I did. But that's just scratching the surface. All of you can do it too if you take your time and think about what you're reading as you read it. It really isn't brain surgery. It's right there in front of you all the time. You just have to look in the right places. That's all.

Now, let's switch gears and take a look at Mr. Frost's poem *The Road Not Taken*, one of my all-time favorites. Like Smith's poem, it is short, though it exceeds Smith's poem by about eight lines and deals with our perception of the world, more specifically a specific scene or image from life. The narrator of the poem is presented with a common image and dilemma: a fork in a path in a forest. One path has clearly been well traveled, meaning that many people have used it. Many have followed the well-trodden path because it is, for the most part, safe. It presents no obstacles. It is easy and clearly marked. This is their perception, and their decision results from it. On the other hand, there is the second path, which is overgrown and unused. It is raw and in its original form.

It represents mystery and possibility as well as uncertainty and danger. And which path does the traveler take?

M: Well, the last line of the poem reads . . . "I took the one less traveled by, and that has made all the difference."

W: Well done. Our traveler chooses the more obscure path by looking past initial perceptions and impressions of uncertainty and solitude toward ones of opportunity and perhaps even adventure. Clearly, the ending is optimistic, making it very different from the dark, pessimistic outcome of Smith's poem. The narrator in Frost's poem looks back on a fulfilling life because he was able to see beyond initial impressions, which is in direct contrast to the drowned person in *Not Waving, But Drowning*. Frost's character seems to be a successful opportunist while Smith's is a failed one. Both poems have the theme of how the surface of things, whether it is of a person's inner nature or nature itself, is just the beginning.

12 Gist-Content Question

Ⓓ The professor focuses on how initial perceptions can be deceptive in discussing both poems.

13 Detail Question

Ⓒ The professor notes, "He tried to mask it by seeming happy, which is symbolized by waving in the title, yet internally, he was in great distress, symbolized by the word "drowning" in the title. Only after death is the person able to vocalize himself and ask for help, but by then it is too late."

14 Making Inferences Question

Ⓑ The professor states, "Personally, I don't believe the person drowned at all, which would be an accident. I don't want to be too morbid, but if the person was as troubled as he seems in the poem, the drowning was probably more on purpose than simply a freak accident."

15 Detail Question

Ⓑ The professor comments, "Our traveler chooses the more obscure path by looking past initial perceptions and impressions of uncertainty and solitude toward ones of opportunity and perhaps even adventure."

16 Connecting Content Question

Smith: [1], [4]   Frost: [2], [3]

About Smith's poem, the professor remarks, "Personally, I don't believe the person drowned at all, which would be an accident. I don't want to be too morbid, but if the person was as troubled as he seems in the poem, the drowning was probably more on purpose than simply a freak accident," and then adds, "Then why is the drowned individual speaking, moaning in the first and last stanzas?" As for Frost's poem, the professor says, "On the other hand, there is the second path, which is overgrown and unused. It is raw and in its original form. It represents mystery and possibility as well as uncertainty and danger," and also states, "Like Smith's poem, it is short, though it exceeds Smith's poem by about eight lines."

17 Understanding Function Question

Ⓐ In stating that analyzing poems is not brain surgery, the professor implies that the students are making their attempts too difficult on themselves.

PART 2 Conversation 🎧 04-04   p.074

W Student: Professor Houston, I'm so glad I caught you in your office. I've been trying to find you all week long. Do you have a minute to speak?

M Professor: Oh, sure, Lucy. Please come in. You've been looking for me?

W: Yes, sir, I have. I've been to your office three times this week, but you weren't here anytime.

M: I'm dreadfully sorry about that. I'm normally pretty good about keeping office hours, but I've had a few personal issues to take care of. Anyway, what can I do for you today?

W: I was hoping to add another class to my schedule, and since you're my advisor, I need to get your permission. The professor for the class has already signed my add slip, so all you need to do is sign it, and then I can take this over to the Registrar's office for someone there to process.

M: Okay. That sounds rather straightforward. So, uh, what is the extra class that you're taking?

W: [4] It's a cultural anthropology class. I figured that I ought to take it now so that I can get my science requirement out of the way completely.

M: Yeah, that makes perfect sense. I remember dreading having to take science classes when I was a student.

W: Well, it's actually pretty interesting, but I still don't have much aptitude with regard to science. So do you think you can sign the paper?

M: Sure, but before I do, can you remind me as to what other classes you're taking this semester?

W: I'm taking two history courses this semester. That's my major, of course. I'm in a math class, too. Oh, I'm also taking Latin 2 with Professor Reid. His class is a load of fun. And this class will give me five courses for the semester. It's a full load, but I know that I can handle the work.

M: Are you sure about that? If I remember correctly, the two history classes that you're enrolled in require a large amount of reading. Professors Marrone and Davidson are not the easiest of graders you know.

W: Hey! You do remember which classes I'm taking. Cool! But to answer your question . . . Yes, these classes will take up a lot of my time, but I've already taken these professors before. I took a class with Professor Marrone my first year here and one with Professor Davidson last semester. So I already know what both of them expect of their students. Plus, I got A's in both of their classes, so I think that proves that I can definitely do the work.

M: [5] That's right. I remember congratulating you on that last semester. Well, it seems like you have all the bases covered. Let me have that form, and I'll give it my signature.

W: Thank you so much, Professor Houston. You know, today is the last day for students to add classes, so I'm really glad that I caught up with you today.

M: In that case, you'd better get over to the Registrar's office now. It's going to close in under thirty minutes.

W: Oh, I guess you're right. See you.

1 Gist-Purpose Question

Ⓐ The student visits the professor to get his permission to take another class.

2 Understanding Attitude Question

Ⓒ The student comments, "Oh, I'm also taking Latin 2 with Professor Reid. His class is a load of fun."

3 Understanding Organization Question

Ⓐ The professor states, "Professors Marrone and Davidson are not the easiest of graders you know."

4 Understanding Function Question

Ⓒ In stating that he dreaded taking science classes, the professor implies that he did not get good grades in them.

5 Understanding Function Question

Ⓑ When the professor says that the student has all the bases covered, he is implying that the student has thought a lot about her classes.

PART 2 Lecture 🎧 04-05   p.077

M Professor: Obviously, muscles are crucial to the human body. Muscles allow us to walk and talk with the help of signals from the brain, and without muscles, we'd basically be big blobs of bones and skin. Now there's a strange image. But let's dig a little deeper into the science of these connective tissues called muscles. Essentially, there are three basic types, which we will attempt to limit our discussion to today and then get into how they function in our next lecture. Okay. Who can name one of them for us?

W Student: How about skeletal muscles?

M: Sure, that's one type . . . It's actually the biggest group in the human body. What I mean is that skeletal muscles populate the human body more than any other kind of muscles. They are responsible for the actual physical movement of our limbs and appendages. They are also the muscles that connect to tendons and ligaments, which connect them to our bones. Another important point about skeletal muscles is that they are voluntary muscles. What do I mean by voluntary? Well, it means that we have, for the most part, conscious control over them. The human body has an entire system devoted exclusively to voluntary muscle control. It's called the somatic nervous system, or SNS, which is actually a branch of the peripheral nervous system, that is, the nervous system in our body outside the brain and spinal cord. We are able to tell them when we want them to start and stop.

And what about their makeup? What do they look like? Well, skeletal muscles are what we call striated muscles. The muscles' fibers are grouped together in crisscrossing band-like fibers and are quite distinct when compared to other muscle tissues. Skeletal muscles comprise the large muscle groups of our bodies. Examples include the latissimus dorsi, the biceps, and the rectus femoris. Another trait of skeletal muscles is their massive blood networks, which are required to feed them with energy. In a way, skeletal muscles are the workhorses of the human body. Now, who can name another type of muscle for us?

W: Another is smooth muscle.

M: You're exactly right, Katie. I take it that you've been doing your reading. Well done. Another major muscle type is called smooth muscle. Examples of smooth muscles can be found in the respiratory tissues, which help us breathe, the intestines, which, well, I think everyone knows what those do, and other major digestive organs. There are more examples of course. Let's take the stomach, for example. Have you ever been sitting in class, perhaps this very one, and all of a sudden your stomach begins to rumble and groan? Well, sure, this is a sign that you're hungry, but it's also a good example of your smooth muscles at work. Your stomach is anticipating food—it's even attempting to jump-start the digestion process—but there isn't much inside the stomach, which is making the embarrassing grumbling sound. Yes, class, that's an example of smooth muscles

at work. But what does this mean? What does this imply? Did you tell your stomach to start churning? Of course not, which brings us to what differentiates smooth muscle from skeletal muscle. It is involuntary and is principally controlled by the autonomic nervous system, also called the ANS, which regulates the continuous function of vital systems in the body such as blood flow and breathing. Further, smooth muscle comes in thin layers of tissue and doesn't contain a heavy mapping of blood vessels, unlike skeletal muscles. Is everyone following me okay? Do you need me to backtrack on anything . . . ? No . . . ? Good. Then who can tell me what the final type of muscle is? Katie again?

W: Well, I know it's heart muscle, but I don't think that's the appropriate term.

M: Actually, you're exactly right, and if we wanted to get really technical, we would call it cardiac muscle. As the name implies, cardiac muscle is the tissue that surrounds the heart and allows it to pump blood throughout our bodies, which is a most critical responsibility. While cardiac muscle is mainly smooth muscle, it also contains a bit of skeletal muscle. Of course, like smooth muscle, it is involuntary as well and is controlled by the ANS. Some experts have found that cardiac muscle will continue to pump blood without any impulses from the brain or the ANS. This is something we'll get more into next class, but I just thought I'd point that out quickly. Of course, like skeletal muscle, cardiac muscle is abundant in blood vessels, as you all can imagine. Yes, a question?

W: Um, I don't want to interrupt your explanation about cardiac muscle, but what about eyelids? I mean, what controls them? They seem to be both voluntary and involuntary, right?

6 Gist-Content Question
  Ⓒ The professor mostly talks about the differences between the three different types of muscles in the body in his lecture.

7 Detail Question
  Ⓐ The professor says, "They are also the muscles that connect to tendons and ligaments, which connect them to our bones."

8 Understanding Organization Question
  Ⓓ The professor remarks, "Skeletal muscles comprise the large muscle groups of our bodies. Examples include the latissimus dorsi, the biceps, and the rectus femoris."

9 Making Inferences Question
  Ⓑ In stating, "Examples of smooth muscles can be found in the respiratory tissues, which help us breathe,"

the professor implies that smooth muscle is critical to the human body.

10 Detail Question

Ⓐ The professor explains, "While cardiac muscle is mainly smooth muscle, it also contains a bit of skeletal muscle."

11 Connecting Content Question

Cardiac: [4] Smooth: [2] Skeletal: [1], [3]

About cardiac muscle, the professor states, "While cardiac muscle is mainly smooth muscle, it also contains a bit of skeletal muscle." Regarding smooth muscle, the professor notes, "Examples of smooth muscles can be found in the respiratory tissues, which help us breath, the intestines, which, well, I think everyone knows what those do, and other major digestive organs." As for skeletal muscle, the professor says, "Skeletal muscles comprise the large muscle groups of our bodies. Examples include the latissimus dorsi, the biceps, and the rectus femoris," and adds, "What I mean is that skeletal muscles populate the human body more than any other kind of muscles."

ACTUAL TEST 05

Answers

PART 1

1	Ⓓ	2	Ⓑ	3	Ⓐ,Ⓒ	4	Ⓐ
5	Ⓐ	6	Ⓒ	7	Ⓑ	8	Ⓑ
9	Ⓐ	10	Bubonic: [2],[4] Pneumonic: [1],[3]				
11	Ⓑ						

PART 2

1	Ⓓ	2	Ⓐ,Ⓑ	3	Ⓒ	4	Ⓒ
5	Ⓐ	6	Ⓒ	7	Ⓑ	8	Ⓑ
9	Ⓐ,Ⓓ	10	Hypersomnia: [3],[4] Insomnia: [1],[2]				
11	Ⓓ	12	Ⓑ	13	Ⓑ	14	Ⓒ
15	Ⓐ	16	Type A: [2],[3] Type B: [1],[4]				
17	Ⓓ						

Scripts & Explanations

PART 1 Conversation 🎧 05-01

M Student Housing Office Employee: Good afternoon. What brings you down to the student housing office?

W Student: Well, I just got the key to my dorm room, and I must say that I'm incredibly disappointed with it. There are so many things wrong with it that I don't even know where to begin.

M: I see. Why don't you have a seat there and tell me what exactly is wrong with your room? To begin with, what's your name, and which dorm are you assigned to?

W: My name is Sheila Patterson. I'm a second-year student here, and I am supposed to live in West Hall. My room number is 407.

M: ⁵Okay. I've got all that information typed into the computer here. According to my records, your room should be in perfect condition. So . . . what exactly is wrong with your dorm room?

W: **Well, there is a whole list of things. I hope you take notes as I speak.** First, when my roommate and I checked in, we discovered that there was only one key. We're supposed to have two . . . you know, one for each of us, but there was just that one.

M: Hmm . . . That happens from time to time. But we can rectify that in a matter of hours. What else is the matter?

W: Okay, uh, so my roommate got into the room. But I had to wait around a couple of hours until Mary showed up with the key. Anyway, once I got in the room, I noticed that there was mold growing both on the walls and in my closet. I couldn't believe it. I thought that you guys had cleaned the rooms thoroughly.

M: Yeah, I don't know what to say to that. It sounds like we need to send someone from Buildings and Grounds over to clean up your room. Well, if that's everything, then I think we can make the necessary arrangements.

W: Actually, I'm not quite yet finished. There's one more problem that came up. Cockroaches. I saw a couple of them in the room. I really think that you need to get someone to fumigate the room for us.

M: Okay. I'll get on that right away. I'm terribly sorry about this. These things just sometimes happen, and you were the unlucky one this year.

W: It's all right. I understand that there are a lot of dormitories, so it's hard to keep track of everything. I do have one request though.

M: Sure. Go ahead and ask.

W: Where can I stay until my room gets cleaned up? I can't stay there with all those problems, and I definitely don't want to be there or even have my stuff in there when the exterminator comes.

M: Good point. Our policy is to put you up in a local hotel until all your problems are solved. We'll also reimburse you for your travel expenses back and forth from the hotel to the school. Just make sure that you keep the receipts for everything.

W: Wow. I wasn't expecting that.

M: Well, we messed up, so the least we can do is make sure that you and your roommate's time away from school is as comfortable as possible.

1 Gist-Content Question

Ⓓ The student's dormitory room is uninhabitable because of the mold and the cockroaches in it.

2 Gist-Purpose Question

Ⓑ The student makes several complaints about her room to the man.

3 Detail Question

Ⓐ, Ⓒ The student says, "Cockroaches. I saw a couple of them in the room," and also adds, "Anyway, once I got in the room, I noticed that there was mold growing both on the walls and in my closet. I couldn't believe it. I thought that you guys had cleaned the rooms thoroughly."

4 Making Inferences Question

Ⓐ In stating, "These things just sometimes happen, and you were the unlucky one this year," the man implies that he has handled similar problems before.

5 Understanding Function Question

Ⓐ In responding, "Well, there is a whole list of things. I hope you take notes as I speak," the student is indicating that there are numerous problems with her dorm room.

PART 1 Lecture   🎧 05-02   p.086

W Professor: There were a number of major causes for the social and religious turmoil experienced in Europe during the fourteenth century. One of the most catastrophic for the people and society as a whole was what is known as the Black Death. Yes, I see that many of you have heard of it. You've probably even studied it before. Well, allow me to give you a quick refresher course on the Black Death, which has come to be known today as the bubonic plague. It originated somewhere in Asia, where it is said to have claimed the lives of around thirty million people, though this number is just an estimate. It could have been much higher . . . Or lower, I suppose. The plague then spread by sea trade, ships, into the Mediterranean and to the island Sicily, where it got its first foothold in Europe. The date of the beginning of its ghastly, horrific assault on Europe was probably around the mid-fourteenth century, most likely 1347 or 1348. Does anyone have any questions or comments at this juncture?

M Student: I do, Professor Stephenson. You mentioned that it is now understood that the Black Death was a kind of bubonic plague. Do you mean there was only one strain of the disease? One type?

W: Well, actually, no. It is generally understood today that the Black Death was essentially a bubonic plague, which is not really the complete story. Allow me to explain. We now know there were two different types of plagues associated with the Black Death in Europe during the time. One was the bubonic plague, as I have mentioned. This was the more common of the two as it affected the greatest number of people. It could only be contracted from fleas or rodents, and it attacked the lymph nodes in the body. It was also the lesser of the two evils since around half of the people who caught it died within a week or so. The second strain was the pneumonic plague, which was probably a mutation of the bubonic plague. It was highly contagious and passed from human to human like wildfire. The pneumonic plague affected the respiratory system, especially the lungs, and it was lethal to all the individuals who were unfortunate enough to contract it. Does that clear things up?

M: Yes, ma'am. Thank you. Um, another quick question. Why did the Black Death spread so quickly? Why couldn't they contain it?

W: Well, I believe the simple answer to that question is that Europe did not realize what it had on its hands until it was too late. But if we look a bit more closely at the conditions in Europe during the time, we can see how Europe was ripe for such an outbreak. First, populations were at an all-time high. Major cities were packed with people basically living on top of one another. City streets were crowded with citizens, and hygiene was not at the top of a fourteenth-century European's list of priorities. ¹¹Garbage and sewage often piled up along city streets and alleys, making them prime spots for the proliferation of bubonic plague-carrying rodents as well. **So you see, uh, the environments of the cities of Europe were primed and ready to host diseases such as the bubonic and pneumonic plagues.** Yes, the filthy living conditions were definitely a major reason why the Black Death was so devastating to Europe. I mean, some accounts claim that disease-ridden corpses were piled up on the streets because coroners would not accept them out of fear of catching the plague themselves.

M: Oh, that's awful. How long did it last?

W: I agree with you. It was a dark time for Europe. Death was more a part of their lives than living. And to answer your question, again, population was everything. The more people there were in a city, the easier it was for the plague to thrive. If the population was sparse, the Black Death would usually run out of steam and run its course within a year. Conversely, densely populated areas could expect it to last for much longer. For the most part, the Black Death did the bulk of its devastation from 1348 to 1430, when it is estimated that around twenty million Europeans succumbed and died from it. That was about one-third of the entire population of Europe back then— one in every three people. Again, some experts believe this number to be a very conservative estimate. When you consider that a city such as Paris, one of the worst affected cities, lost about half of its population, you can realize how cataclysmic the effects of the Black Death were on Europe at the time.

6 Gist-Content Question

Ⓒ The professor mostly talks about the onset of the Black Death and how it spread.

7 Understanding Organization Question

Ⓑ The professor states, "The plague then spread by sea trade, ships, into the Mediterranean and to the island Sicily, where it got its first foothold in Europe."

8 Making Inferences Question

Ⓑ In stating, "The second strain was the pneumonic plague, which was probably a mutation of the bubonic plague," the professor implies that the pneumonic plague was spawned by the bubonic plague.

9 Detail Question

Ⓐ The professor lectures, "The more people there were in a city, the easier it was for the plague to thrive. If the population was sparse, the Black Death would usually run out of steam and run its course within a year. Conversely, densely populated areas could expect it to last for much longer."

10 Connecting Content Question

Bubonic: 2, 4 Pneumonic: 1, 3

About the bubonic plague, the professor states, "One was the bubonic plague, as I have mentioned. This was the more common of the two as it affected the greatest number of people. It could only be contracted from fleas or rodents." As for the pneumonic plague, the professor notes, "The second strain was the pneumonic plague, which was probably a mutation of the bubonic plague. It was highly contagious and passed from human to human like wildfire. The pneumonic plague affected the respiratory system, especially the lungs, and it was lethal to all the individuals who were unfortunate enough to contract it."

11 Understanding Function Question

Ⓑ In stating, "So you see, uh, the environments of the cities of Europe were primed and ready to host diseases such as the bubonic and pneumonic plagues," the professor implies that cleaner lifestyles could have reduced the harm caused during the Black Plague.

PART 2 Conversation 🎧 05-03   p.089

W Student: Oh, Professor Stevens. I'm glad I caught you. Are you going home because I want to talk with you a bit about my schedule next semester if I could?

M Professor: Well, Angela, I was actually on my way home, but I can spare a few moments for you. Shoot!

W: Oh, great. Thanks, Professor. Well, I was planning on taking Dr. Whitlam's humanities seminar. Do you think that is a good choice?

M: I believe that is an excellent choice. Even though he has only been here for a couple of years, I hear that his lectures are quite animated and lively. He still has that zest for instruction if you get my meaning. I do know that he can be quite demanding, too, which might turn off a lot of students.

W: Yes. A friend of mine had him, and she said the same thing. I like challenging courses, so I think I would enjoy his. Great. Now, what about Professor Rice? Do you know her?

M: Of course I do, Angela. She's the chair of the Religion Department. I believe she has a class on early Christianity next fall. Actually, she has been a good friend of mine for many years, and I consider her to be a topnotch lecturer and authority on Western religions. Therefore, that's another excellent pick in my opinion, Angela.

W: [5] Wonderful! I haven't taken any classes in religion yet, but I'm really looking forward to hers. I just hope it isn't full by the time I register. **Usually, all the seniors and juniors fill the good classes up first.**

M: Well, if that happens, come and talk to me, and perhaps I can put in a good word for you. How does that sound? I wouldn't want you to miss out on her class.

W: Wow, thanks for going out of your way for me, sir. That is very generous of you. Okay, um, I'm not keeping you too long, am I, because I need just a little bit more advice if you can?

M: No problem, Angela. Ask away.

W: Well, the final class I want to ask you about is yours, sir. You're teaching the folklore class, right? Yes, um, I was wondering if you were going to include any Zora Neale Hurston in the reading. She is one of my favorite African-American writers, and I was just hoping . . .

M: Oh, so you've been reading Zora, huh? Well, that is wonderful. Actually, no folklore class would be complete without exploring at least some of her work. I believe the early part of the class will focus on Hurston, and then we'll branch out into other examples from the South. I'm in the process of reorganizing the syllabus, so I'm just not sure of the exact path we will take, but I can assure you that she will be one of the major writers we discuss.

W: Oh, that's great, sir! And I'm sorry for taking up so much of your time. I'll let you know about the religion class, and I guess I'll see you soon. Thanks again. Bye.

1 Gist-Content Question

Ⓓ The speakers are mainly talking about the professor's opinion on some classes the student is interested in taking.

2 Detail Question

Ⓐ, Ⓑ The professor remarks, "I hear that his lectures are quite animated and lively. He still has that zest for instruction if you get my meaning. I do know that he can be quite demanding, too, which might turn off a lot of students."

3 Making Inferences Question

Ⓒ In stating, "I consider her to be a topnotch lecturer and authority on Western religions," the professor implies that Professor Rice does not specialize in religions from Africa.

4 Detail Question

Ⓒ About Zora Neale Hurston, the professor comments, "Actually, no folklore class would be complete without exploring at least some of her work."

5 Understanding Function Question

Ⓐ In stating, "Usually, all the seniors and juniors fill the good classes up first," the student is indicating that the school's registration policy benefits upperclassmen.

PART 2 Lecture #1 🎧 05-04   p.092

M Professor: There are a number of sleeping disorders, and while the large majority of them stem from psychological causes, a couple of them are actually physiological disorders that usually have their origins in the brain. One of the most common sleep issues that many people face every day is what is called hypersomnia, which I'm sure most of you have heard of and perhaps some of you have, unfortunately, experienced.

W Student: Uh, don't you mean insomnia, Professor Jenkins?

M: Well, no, to be honest. I'm sure many of you were expecting me to say insomnia, but I'm going to save that for the next segment of my lecture this morning. First, I'd like to talk about what is known as hypersomnia. Contrary to popular belief, many studies have shown that hypersomnia could actually be even more common than its nocturnal cousin, insomnia. Now, the prefix *hyper* obviously suggests excessive or beyond the limits, which tells us that a person who is suffering from hypersomnia gets too much sleep or has the inability to keep awake. This is the complete opposite of insomnia. It is the need to sleep during the daytime even after one has had a full night or more of quality sleeping time. Is everyone following me out there? Is everyone awake . . . ? Sorry, poor joke. Very poor joke. Anyway, who knows what the name of the condition of an extreme form of hypersomnia is? Anybody?

W: [11] Sorry, Professor Jenkins. I pulled an all-nighter last night. Um, that would be narcolepsy, sir. The, um, answer to your question.

M: Very good. And thank you for making it in to class this morning. She's right, too, class. Narcolepsy is an extreme form of hypersomnia. In the case of narcolepsy, the individual has no ability whatsoever to control when he falls asleep. It only occurs during the daytime. For example, if a friend of yours is stricken by narcolepsy, you could be having a lively conversation with him, but suddenly, he essentially passes out and falls asleep. Narcoleptics can suddenly fall into a deep sleep. Depending on the episode, the individual could be asleep for five minutes or even longer than an hour. There is really no warning as to its onset either. Occasionally, the episode may be preceded by some visible drowsiness, but it usually just hits out of nowhere. Scientists believe that narcolepsy is a genetic disorder passed down through generations, and it is a condition in which the brain is unable properly to regulate when sleep should occur. Still, there is no known cure for it. It is not directly life threatening but you can imagine what would happen if a narcoleptic were driving a car or piloting a plane when an episode suddenly materializes.

W: Ouch!

M: Exactly. So now you know why it's important to diagnose this condition early before something terrible happens. Sometimes a change in diet, as in eating more vegetables while consuming less meat, can help reduce the symptoms, and occasionally doctors provide stimulants, but these can cause addiction and are usually avoided except in the most extreme cases.

Now, the second disorder, which we've already determined is insomnia, is a condition in which the individual has trouble falling asleep or wakes up repeatedly during the night. Its causes are usually psychological in the form of stress, depression, and too much worrying, but other external causes, such as caffeinated drinks and smoking, are often culprits as well because they are stimulants. Additionally, if you take too many naps during the day . . . How wonderful that would be . . . ? Your body might become too well rested, uh, if that's possible, and cause the onset of sleeplessness. Now the obvious effects of insomnia are fatigue and a lack of energy during the day. That is to be expected; yet another underlying problem comes in the form of a weakened immune system. When you don't sleep enough at night, your body loses the opportunity to repair itself, to rejuvenate, you know, and the immune system usually suffers the most, resulting in numerous problems.

There are a few tactics you can use to ensure a good night's sleep. One is to keep a regular schedule by going to bed and waking up at the same times, which will program your circadian rhythm, your internal clock, and help you fall asleep and stay asleep. Of course, avoiding coffee, soft drinks, and even alcohol in the evenings is another step. For individuals who still suffer from insomnia, some people swear by hypnosis techniques. Further, a popular natural remedy that is also used for jet lag is melatonin, which helps restore the body's natural rhythms and timings. Of course, doctors can also prescribe sleeping aid medications, but these can have terrible side effects, and the individual always runs the risk of becoming psychologically dependent on them. That's not a good thing and should be avoided unless absolutely necessary.

6 Gist-Content Question

Ⓒ The professor mostly lectures on the causes of two major sleeping disorders.

7 Detail Question

Ⓑ About narcolepsy, the professor states, "Narcolepsy is an extreme form of hypersomnia. In the case of narcolepsy, the individual has no ability whatsoever to control when he falls asleep. It only occurs during the daytime."

8 Making Inferences Question

Ⓑ The professor remarks, "Yet another underlying problem comes in the form of a weakened immune system. When you don't sleep enough at night, your body loses the opportunity to repair itself, to rejuvenate, you know, and the immune system usually suffers the most, resulting in numerous problems." It can therefore be implied that a person suffering from it is prone to getting illnesses and diseases.

9 Detail Question

Ⓐ, Ⓓ The professor notes, "Of course, doctors can also prescribe sleeping aid medications, but these can have terrible side effects, and the individual always runs the risk of becoming psychologically dependent on them. That's not a good thing and should be avoided unless absolutely necessary."

10 Connecting Content Question

Hypersomnia: ③, ④ Insomnia: ①, ②

About hypersomnia, the professor states, "Sometimes a change in diet, as in eating more vegetables while consuming less meat, can help reduce the symptoms," and adds, "Scientists believe that narcolepsy is a genetic disorder passed down through generations." Regarding insomnia, the professor notes, "Further, a popular natural remedy that is also used for jet lag is melatonin, which helps restore the body's natural rhythms and timings," and adds, "One is to keep a regular schedule by going to bed and waking up at the same times, which will program your circadian rhythm, your internal clock, and help you fall asleep and stay asleep."

11 Understanding Function Question

Ⓓ In stating, "Sorry, Professor Jenkins. I pulled an all-nighter last night," the student is noting that she could not sleep because she had to study last night.

PART 2 Lecture #2   🎧 05-05   p.095

M Professor: How about if everyone stands up for a second? Come on. Don't be shy. Great. Now take a look around the lecture hall at everyone. Do you notice anything? Think body types, guys.

W Student: Everyone looks like they need a couple of cups of coffee.

M: Or maybe you guys need to try to exercise more. Okay. Go ahead and take a seat now. Well, what I was trying to do with my little experiment is to show you that we all come in various shapes and sizes. In general, an individual's body type can fit into one of three general categories: endomorph, ectomorph, and mesomorph. These are called somatotypes, and for the most part, each one of our bodies, as well as our character or personality, can be categorized as one of them. Have you heard of somatotypes before . . . ? No? Well, our body types are usually fixed by heredity, that is, genetics.

For example, if you are tall and thin, it is pretty much impossible to change physically. If you are short and have large bones, that is how you will look for much of your life. Our bone and muscle structures as well as their densities are predetermined by our genes. Now, this doesn't mean you cannot shape your body to be a more desirable look. Proper exercise and diet can certainly max out the potential of whatever body type you might be, but still, inside, you will remain that body type in essence. Does this make sense to you guys?

W: Sure, Professor Nelson. So what are the three body types?

M: Well, how about if you do me a favor and stand up again for the class? Great. Thanks. Now, everyone, take a look at her body. Okay . . . Now, we would probably describe her as taller than average and a bit thin. Correct? Okay, uh, you can go ahead and sit down. Because she is tall and a bit on the lean side, we would say she is an ectomorph. Be sure to take all this down, guys. There will be a quiz on it tomorrow. I promise. Now, in general, ectomorphs also sometimes—but not all the time—display similar personality characteristics. They tend to be type B personalities and are a bit reserved or shy, sensitive, and emotional. Now, if you would describe yourself as an ectomorph and your personality fits what I have just described, please raise your hand. Great. Thank you. Okay, uh, let's move on to the second somatotype. Let me see . . . You in the purple polo shirt up here in the front. Could you stand up for me, please? Um, turn around for us a couple of times. Great. Thanks. Go ahead and take your seat. Thanks. Now, class, how would you describe his body?

W: Well, I think he looks great! He's got a great build and isn't too short or tall.

M: And I think most of us would agree with you. We would say he is a mesomorph. Mesomorphs have very athletic builds. Their bone and muscle structures are well balanced, and their body fat percentage is low. I guess you could say that mesomorphs have an athletic build. When it comes to somatotypes, class, it is all about proportions. Clearly, he has a very well-proportioned body and probably works out or exercises religiously. Am I correct . . . ? Yes, I thought so. Now, what about the stereotypical personality of the mesomorph? Well, again, in general, they are type A personalities. They are very energetic and outgoing, and they also tend to be very confident in themselves and their abilities. [17] Now, that leaves one more somatotype to explore, and I've saved this one for myself. It's only fair, right, class, that you critique my body as well, right? **So here I am. Have at it!**

W: Well, Professor Nelson, you are a bit short and probably need to exercise more or try to cut back on the fast food or something. Sorry, sir.

M: Oh, there is no reason to be, and I thank you for your honesty. Class, her description is right on the money. I am what you would describe as an endomorph. Endomorphs are typically shorter than average, have larger bones, and tend to be more overweight than the average person. When it comes to personality, they are very sociable, relaxed, fun loving, and compassionate, all of which I would definitely describe myself as. Okay, uh, now that we have defined the three somatotypes, I'd like to discuss the different techniques of exercise each body type should be involved in on a regular basis to try to make their proportions more equal, and yes, this goes for mesomorphs, too. While mesomorphs may seem perfect, their seemingly ultimate body type can sometimes lead to their downfall.

12 Gist-Content Question
Ⓑ The lecture is mostly about the three basic somatotypes.

13 Detail Question
Ⓑ The professor tells the class, "Well, our body types are usually fixed by heredity, that is, genetics."

14 Making Inferences Question
Ⓒ The professor implies throughout his lecture that certain body types often have similar personalities.

15 Detail Question
Ⓐ The professor says, "Well, again, in general, they are type A personalities. They are very energetic and outgoing, and they also tend to be very confident in themselves and their abilities."

16 Connecting Content Question
Type A: ②, ③ Type B: ①, ④

About type A personalities, the professor says, "Well, again, in general, they are type A personalities. They are very energetic and outgoing, and they also tend to be very confident in themselves and their abilities." As for type B personalities, the professor notes, "They tend to be type B personalities and are a bit reserved or shy, sensitive, and emotional."

17 Understanding Attitude Question
Ⓓ When the professor says, "So here I am. Have at it!" it can be inferred that he is enthusiastic about being an example for the students.

ACTUAL TEST 06

Answers

PART 1

1. D
2. A
3. Fact: 1, 3 Not a Fact: 2, 4
4. C
5. A
6. C
7. B
8. C
9. C
10. Fortunato: 1, 4 Montresor: 2, 3
11. D

PART 2

1. A
2. A
3. D
4. C
5. B
6. C
7. B
8. A
9. B
10. Weather Forecast: 1, 3 Earthquake Forecast: 2, 4
11. C
12. A
13. C
14. B
15. B
16. Fulton: 2, 3 Shreve: 1, 4
17. B

Scripts & Explanations

PART 1 Conversation 🎧 06-01

W Building Administrator: Hello. Would you happen to be Artis Coleman?

M Student: That's right. I'm afraid I don't know you though. Can I help you with something?

W: Actually, I believe I'm the one who can help you. I'm Julie Dawson, and I am the administrator of Montana Hall.

M: Oh, yes, you can help me out for sure. I've been trying to speak with you quite frequently for the past couple of days. I'm so glad you managed to make my life easier by finding me.

W: I'm very sorry about that. Every time you visited my office, I was either in a meeting with someone or in another building. But I found out who your advisor is and contacted her. Professor Sanderson told me that you'd probably be in Richardson Hall, so I came over here to see if I could talk to you.

M: It's my lucky day. I really appreciate your making the extra effort.

W: It's not a problem at all. Now, uh, what can I help you with?

M: I'm the president of one of the drama clubs on campus. The name of our club is the Royal Players. Have you heard of us?

W: I'm afraid not. I thought I knew every drama club at the school, but yours is a new one to me.

M: We just started in the fall semester, so this is only our second semester in existence. Anyway, we focused solely on our acting techniques during the fall semester, but we've gained some experience and a few new members, so we're ready to perform a play this semester.

W: And you need to find out from me when you can use the auditorium, right?

M: Yes, that's correct. We're hoping to put on our play in the last two weeks of April, preferably on a weekend night. Would you happen to know off the top of your head if that's possible?

W: Unfortunately, every weekend in April—by that, I mean Friday and Saturday nights—is completely booked by other drama clubs or by the members of the Drama or Music departments.

M: Oh, that's too bad.

W: Nevertheless, there are plenty of other dates available.

M: What would you recommend?

W: It's not really up to me. It's your choice.

M: Yes, but, well, I've never done this before, so I thought I would ask you. Basically, we want a night that will be convenient for our friends and relatives as well as a few students who might be interested in attending the show.

W: Hmm . . . How many props are you going to have?

M: Props? Not too many. We also have some people who will do the lighting, the curtains, and all of the other stage work.

W: Ah, that's great. In that case, I would suggest a Thursday night. Those nights are often fairly well attended by students, and Thursday is close enough to the weekend that friends and family members can visit campus to see the show.

M: That sounds great. Which Thursday nights in April are available?

W: I don't happen to recall that information. Why don't we head over to my office right now so that we can find out? Then, you can make the reservation, and I can talk to you about what is required of student groups that use the auditorium in Montana Hall.

1. **Gist-Content Question**

   Ⓓ The woman says, "Every time you visited my office, I was either in a meeting with someone or in another building. But I found out who your advisor is and contacted her. Professor Sanderson told me that you'd probably be in Richardson Hall, so I came over here to see if I could talk to you."

2. **Making Inferences Question**

   Ⓐ When the student says, "I've been trying to speak with you quite frequently for the past couple of days," it can be inferred that he was unable to meet the woman yesterday.

3. **Connecting Content Question**

   Fact: ①, ③ Not a Fact: ②, ④

   The student says, "The name of our club is the Royal Players," and then adds, "We just started in the fall semester, so this is only our second semester in existence." Those are facts. However, he states, "Anyway, we focused solely on our acting techniques during the fall semester, but we've gained some experience and a few new members, so we're ready to perform a play this semester," so the club has not performed a play before. In addition, he notes, "We also have some people who will do the lighting, the curtains, and all of the other stage work," so the club does not need help managing the stage.

4. **Detail Question**

   Ⓒ The woman comments, "I would suggest a Thursday night."

5. **Making Inferences Question**

   Ⓐ The woman states, "Why don't we head over to my office right now so that we can find out?"

PART 1 Lecture 🎧 06-02   p.104

M Professor: Now, to wrap up our session today, we will begin discussing Poe's short story *The Cask of Amontillado*. I gather that everyone has read the story, right . . . ? Wonderful! Please remember to focus on the basics when you study literature, class. Focus on the setting, the characters, the plot, and the theme. Pay particular attention to details, especially with regard to Poe's work, because they are always there for a reason. They help us find the deeper meaning as well as Poe's specific intentions in his poetry and stories. Let's take a brief look now at the setting of the story, then we'll look at the characters, and then, if we have time, we'll discuss some of the themes. So . . . uh, what's the setting?

W Student: The story starts out at a kind of festival or carnival, and then it shifts to the catacombs.

M: [11] That's correct. Oh, and are we all clear on what catacombs are, everyone . . . ? No? I'm seeing a lot of blank faces out there. Traditionally they are a kind of underground cemetery that are found in places like Italy and France. They are cold, dark, and musty and are where people would entomb dead family members. Does that clear it up . . . ? Perfect. Now, I believe that there is another minor setting of the story. Anyone?

W: Ah, right. On their way to the catacombs, they stop by Montresor's home, right, sir?

M: Very good. His home, or villa, is significant because it gives us some insight into Montresor's family, his roots, as the vaults of his ancestors lie just underneath his grand home. The setting here also helps us distinguish between the background of our two main characters, Montresor and Fortunato. Clearly, Montresor is from the old guard. He is a nobleman with an extensive lineage. We know this because there is a family seal, called a coat of arms on the wall in the catacombs. It suggests that Montresor's family is upper class and important. In contrast, we have Fortunato. What does the name itself suggest to you class?

W Maybe fortune or fortunate? Lucky?

M: Well, done. Poe gives us a hint about Fortunato's own history in his name itself: fortunate. Fortunato, like Montresor, is probably wealthy, yet he is most likely a member of the nouveau riche, that is, the newly rich. His family, his ancestors, never had any real money, yet he has come into a recent fortune. Let's make this distinction clear, class. Montresor is of noble blood while Fortunato is of the aristocracy but only due to monetary wealth. He was not born into it. Fortunato gained his wealth by chance, not by birth or hard work. Is everyone following me . . . ? Good. Now let's continue with this contrast of the two main characters. How are they dressed in the story? Remember that the story starts during the night carnival in, probably, Rome.

W: "He had on a tight-fitting parti-striped dress, and his head was surmounted by the conical cap and bells." That's from the beginning, sir.

M: Excellent. Notice how Poe is setting up the contrast between characters early on in the story, class. Fortunato is in some kind of spandex-like dress, and he has bells on his head. Now, this might remind you of a jester or even a woman. Therefore, Fortunato looks very much like a fool or even an imposter; that is, he might have wealth, but, essentially, he is a clown, a fake. Poe continues this technique of making Fortunato look like a fool throughout the story as well. Later in the story, when he talks, his bells jingle on top of his head. These images are meant to enforce how he is both pitiful and foolish. Does everyone agree with this assessment . . . ?

Now, how about Montresor? How is he dressed, and what does it suggest? Anyone . . . ? Can anyone remember what Montresor is wearing in the story? Well, let me remind you, class, that you should always pay attention to the details. Now, old Montresor is wearing both a dark full-length cloak and a black silk mask. What does this imply, class? What does the mask symbolize to you?

W: Oh, I've got it! Montresor is dressed like an executioner!

M: That's exactly right. Well done. So on one side we have Fortunato dressed very much like a fool, and on the other is Montresor in his ominous executioner's garb. Remember, class, that this is clearly intentional by Poe to separate the characters from one another as well as to show the reader who is in control. Oh, I believe that is all the time we have today, class. On Wednesday, we will continue with the story by discussing its major themes, and we'll also explore what and why certain things occur down in the dark catacombs.

6 Gist-Content Question

Ⓒ The professor makes a comparison of the two main characters in the story.

7 Detail Question

Ⓑ The professor notes, "Let's make this distinction clear, class. Montresor is of noble blood while Fortunato is of the aristocracy but only due to monetary wealth."

8 Detail Question

Ⓒ The professor lectures, "He was not born into it. Fortunato gained his wealth by chance, not by birth or hard work."

9 Making Inferences Question

Ⓒ In stating, "So on one side we have Fortunato dressed very much like a fool, and on the other is Montresor in his ominous executioner's garb," the professor implies that Montressor will kill Fortunato.

10 Connecting Content Question

Fortunato: 1, 4   Montresor: 2, 3

About Fortunato, the professor states, "Later in the story, when he talks, his bells jingle on top of his head, and adds, "Fortunato, like Montresor, is probably wealthy, yet he is most likely a member of the nouveau riche." As for Montresor, the professor remarks, "Clearly, Montresor is from the old guard. He is a nobleman with an extensive lineage. We know this because there is a family seal, called a coat of arms on the wall in the catacombs. It suggests that Montresor's family is upper class and important."

11 Understanding Function Question

Ⓓ When the professor says that he sees blank faces, he is noting that he believes the students do not completely understand his lecture.

PART 2 Conversation 🎧 06-03   p.107

W Professor: Um, Jonathan, can you come in here for a second? I'd like to discuss your final paper topic with you.

M Student: Sure, Professor Briggs. What did you think?

W: Well, Oliver Stone has been beaten to death. I do, however, like your idea about Bono and how he has turned into a human rights activist over the years. Maybe you could explore how he has changed over the years from simply being a music icon into this kind of save-the-globe international entity.

M: Yeah, that might work, ma'am. Thanks for the idea. By the way, how long does the final paper have to be?

W: Well, that's really up to you. I didn't put a firm word count on it. I want you guys to decide that on your own. Typically, though, to give you an idea, final papers for this class average between eight and ten pages. [5] That doesn't mean your paper can't be four or five pages long though. Just make sure it is well organized, well written, and well argued. **I don't want any fluff in these papers.** You guys should know what you are doing at this point.

M: I see. And, um, could you also remind me as to what percentage of the final grade it is?

W: Jonathan, didn't we go over this in class? And I know for a fact it is all explained clearly on your syllabus.

M: I know. But, actually, the other day, I left both my text and all my notes in the coffee shop by Janson Hall, and by the time I realized I had left them there and gone back, they weren't there anymore. I asked the waitress and the manager if they happened to have picked them up, but they said no. They said they'd keep an eye out for them though.

W: I'm sorry to hear that, but you must be more careful. This has happened before, hasn't it?

M: Oh, I know. I can be very forgetful when I have a lot on my mind like I have lately.

W: I understand. I tell you what. If you can't find your notes by tomorrow, come back here, and I'll see if I can help you out one way or another. Anyway, the final paper is forty percent of your final grade.

M: That would be great! So do you think Bono is a good topic for the paper? Is it okay if I borrow your idea on how to organize it, ma'am?

W: Sure. That's why I suggested it to you although I'm sure you would have come up with that on your own, right?

M: Okay. Well, maybe I'll see you tomorrow, but I really appreciate your help, oh, and advice, Professor. Sometimes I just need a little nudge in the right direction. That's all. Anyway, I really appreciate how you look out for me every now and then.

W: Don't worry about it. That's what I'm here for. Again, if you need anything else, just stop by tomorrow. I'll be in my office until six.

1 Gist-Purpose Question

Ⓐ The professor makes a suggestion about the topic of the student's paper.

2 Making Inferences Question

Ⓐ In stating, "This has happened before, hasn't it?" the professor is implying that the student's mind tends to wander.

3 Detail Question

Ⓓ The student tells the professor, "But, actually, the other day, I left both my text and all my notes in the coffee shop by Janson Hall, and by the time I realized I had left them there and gone back, they weren't there anymore."

4 Understanding Attitude Question

Ⓒ The professor offers to help the student several times, so she is somewhat protective of him.

5 Understanding Function Question

Ⓑ In stating, "I don't want any fluff in these papers," she implies that some students include unimportant information in their papers.

PART 2 Lecture #1 🎧 06-04   p.110

M Professor: Well, when it comes to actually predicting an earthquake, it is a very hazy area. Most earthquakes occur without any warning at all. Let's take California, for example. It is basically a patchwork of different fault lines. For example, the Hayward Fault is located in the San Francisco area of California, well, Berkeley, to be exact. Actually, the original architects of the University of California at Berkeley built the campus directly on top of the fault if you can believe that one. The fault itself splits the campus right in half. Luckily, they had the presence of mind to factor in a potential quake in the design of the campus even way back in the early 1900s.

According to records, the Hayward Fault has not experienced a quake since the late 1800s, which is, in a sense, worrisome to many experts as well as residents. To them, it has been quiet for way too long and could be the center of one of California's next devastating quakes. We must remember, class, that even though there have been major technological advances over the past few years in measurement devices as well as new theories on how and why earthquakes occur, even the most experienced and esteemed experts cannot—I repeat: cannot—predict when an earthquake will occur. Now, let me go ahead and take this a step further. Many experts have not given up, but for the time being, they have resorted to making what they call earthquake forecasts, much like a weather forecast, which attempt to predict a window during which an earthquake is most likely to occur. Now, uh, to continue with our weather forecast analogy, what sort of window do they usually fall under?

W Student: Most of the weather forecasts on television and on the Internet predict local weather for a week or so.

M: That's about right. Weather forecasters can take a look at the doppler radar in order to see with their own eyes what the weather conditions are like virtually anywhere in the world right now and what is on the way. So they can try to determine what the weather will be like, for example, on the weekend. Now, are they always right on the money? Of course not. But they are able to give us a general idea of what to expect. There is some degree of accuracy to it.

Now, let's get back to our earthquake experts, whom we also call seismologists. In the past few decades, a few of them, both in the United States and in other countries, have attempted to make earthquake forecasts. As an example, let's say that a Dr. Smith has predicted there will be a major earthquake in the so-and-so area within the next five years. Well, that is a pretty broad range now, isn't it? [11] Many other experts would not touch something like that with a ten-foot pole if you get what I mean. **They realize that trying to predict an earthquake is like shooting darts blindfolded.** Right now, with how little we know about earthquakes, it simply isn't possible.

Now, that doesn't mean that seismologists don't understand where they come from. Advances in what has come to be known as plate tectonics, that is, the study of continental drift and how mountains and volcanoes form, have been huge in the past century. Let's take, for example, another major fault in California. It's arguably the most famous one in the world: the San Andreas Fault. Scientists now know that it is a six or seven-hundred-mile-long fault line extending from San Francisco all the way down south of L.A. and is the area where the Pacific and North American plates slowly grind past one another at a rate of about two inches per year. Sure, um, they can measure the movement of the plates but not when it will spawn an earthquake and where. The area is just too broad. There are infinite possibilities, which can be very frustrating to seismologists, especially when a single earthquake can potentially cause more damage and loss of life in a few seconds than five hurricanes over the course of a day or so. The pressure, no pun intended, class, is huge.

So what's the problem? Well, for one thing, it is difficult for scientists to see what is going on inside the Earth or a fault underground. It is difficult—actually impossible, so far—for them to take a snapshot, unlike the meteorologist and the weather, of a fault underneath the surface, where things are happening and churning. For the most part, their deductions have had to be made from surface perceptions, which are not nearly enough. But this is changing as experts have begun drilling deep into the ground to attain better data and to explore the inner workings of various faults, such as the San Andreas, which has been found to extend more than two miles down.

6 Gist-Content Question

Ⓒ The professor mostly talks about the difficulty involved in predicting earthquakes.

7 Understanding Organization Question

Ⓑ In discussing weather prediction, the professor contrasts it with earthquake prediction.

8 Detail Question

Ⓐ The professor states, "It's arguably the most famous one in the world: the San Andreas Fault."

9 Making Inferences Question

Ⓑ In stating, "Well, for one thing, it is difficult for scientists to see what is going on inside the Earth or a fault underground. It is difficult—actually impossible, so far—for them to take a snapshot, unlike the meteorologist and the weather, of a fault underneath the surface, where things are happening and churning. For the most part, their deductions have had to be made from surface perceptions, which are not nearly enough," the professor implies that earthquake prediction is not an accurate science.

10 Connecting Content Question

Weather Forecast: 1, 3   Earthquake Forecast: 2, 4
About weather forecasts, the professor states, "Weather forecasters can take a look at the doppler radar in order to see with their own eyes what the weather conditions are like virtually anywhere in the world right now and what is on the way. So they can try to determine what the weather will be like, for example, on the weekend. Now, are they always right on the money? Of course not. But they are able to give us a general idea of what to expect. There is some degree of accuracy to it." As for earthquake forecasts, the professor notes, "Many other experts would not touch something like that with a ten-foot pole if you get what I mean. They realize that trying to predict an earthquake is like shooting darts blindfolded. Right now, with how little we know about earthquakes, it simply isn't possible."

11 Understanding Function Question

Ⓒ In stating, "They realize that trying to predict an earthquake is like shooting darts blindfolded," the professor is showing the futility of trying to predict earthquakes.

PART 2 Lecture #2   🎧 06-05   p.113

W Professor: Steam travel finally became a viable means of transportation in the United States in the late eighteenth and early nineteenth centuries. Steamboats became the first vehicles to take advantage of this new form of power, and they were fundamental in igniting growth and industry in the United States along its major rivers and waterways, such as the Mississippi River. In the early nineteenth century, steamboats became the means for commerce for a couple of reasons. One was speed, which I'll talk about in a bit. Second was the fact that upstream travel finally became a reality. Sure, it's true that riverboat commerce and trade existed before the steamboat, but they were completely controlled by the currents, that is, the direction of the flow of the river. Steamboats made it possible to travel both down and back up a river against the flow, a complete roundtrip if you will. Because of this, the steamboat became a huge contributor to the U.S. economy by transporting supplies such as sugar and machinery from east to west as well as from north to south along the Mississippi River and its estuaries.

In addition, thanks to the steamboat, numerous towns, industries, and jobs began to sprout up along the rivers, making it a very prosperous and ambitious time. I'm sure most of you have read Mark Twain's *Life on the Mississippi*, correct? Well, his accounts are quite accurate, I might add, considering he was a licensed riverboat captain. These steamboats must have been something to behold on the rivers due to their size and elaborate, even luxurious, construction and appearance. They were the gems of the river, and their captains were, if you will pardon my metaphor, class, superstars. But they truly were.

M Student: Why superstars, ma'am?

W: Well, think about it for a second. They were the ones in control, the ones who harnessed and manipulated the massive boats and the powerful steam engines. Most people were used to seeing small paddleboats or canoes. When they saw a gigantic steamboat, and if they were lucky, its captain, I'm sure they were simply in awe of the entire scene. Now, one of the earliest superstars, as I have dubbed these steamboat captains, was Robert Fulton. He was one of the first to take a steamboat from Pittsburgh to New Orleans via the Ohio River and Mississippi in 1807. Though the trip was successful, later ones revealed his ship's engineering needed a lot of improvement. It was vastly underpowered and slow.

A more successful captain was Henry Shreve of the *Washington*, which started its runs around 1815. [17] Shreve took his steamboat for a 1,400-mile trip, which took about three weeks. Usually, the same journey would have taken months by any other means. Their speed of travel made steamboats the most attractive and practical option for shipping as well as human travel. **By the way, this same 1,400-mile trip took a mere four days forty years later.** So speed was a major reason for the popularity of steamboats. Two others, especially to people, were their elaborate, luxurious designs and accommodations. Class, these steamboats were literally floating palaces equipped with chandeliers, saloons, dining rooms with white linen on the tables and silverware, the works. Obviously, only the wealthy could afford to pay for passage on the steamboat, and it is clear that the top ones had much in common with the most luxurious ocean liners later on such as the *Titanic*. Yes, class, this is the level of luxury and accommodations we are dealing with here.

What else? Let me see . . . Most of the ships were over two hundred and fifty or even three hundred feet long. Some of the largest ones could even carry over 1,000 passengers. They were clearly grand, large-scale affairs. But they weren't perfect. One of the most common problems with the steamboat was fire, especially considering that steamboats were made out of wood. Another one, very much associated with and usually the cause of most fires, was boiler room explosions. The popularity of the steamboat was, unfortunately, short lived. By 1854, the newly invented railroad was beginning to gain speed. Initially, it helped steamboat trade by bringing goods and supplies from east to west and by loading steamboats for northerly and southerly trips along the rivers. But, sadly, by the 1870s, the railroad had all but replaced steamboats, and they experienced a rapid decline in favor of railroads for both supplies and passengers. Soon, railways were being laid not only east to west but also north to south, and because the railroad was more efficient and frequent as well as more reliable timewise, it quickly became the dominant mode of transportation in the United States and helped the country expand even more swiftly to the west coast.

12 Gist-Content Question

Ⓐ The professor mostly talks about the changes that the steamboat created in the United States.

13 Detail Question

Ⓒ The professor points out, "Because of this, the steamboat became a huge contributor to the U.S. economy by transporting supplies such as sugar and machinery from east to west as well as from north to south along the Mississippi River and its estuaries."

14 Gist-Purpose Question

Ⓑ The professor states, "Obviously, only the wealthy could afford to pay for passage on the steamboat, and it is clear that the top ones had much in common with the most luxurious ocean liners later on such as the *Titanic*. Yes, class, this is the level of luxury and accommodations we are dealing with here."

15 Detail Question

Ⓑ The professor comments, "Soon, railways were being laid not only east to west but also north to south, and, because the railroad was more efficient and frequent as well as more reliable timewise, it quickly became the dominant mode of transportation in the United States and helped the country expand even more swiftly to the west coast."

16 Connecting Content Question

Fulton: ②, ③ Shreve: ①, ④

About Captain Fulton, the professor states, "He was one of the first to take a steamboat from Pittsburgh to New Orleans via the Ohio River and Mississippi in 1807. Though the trip was successful, later ones revealed his ship's engineering needed a lot of improvement." As for Captain Shreve, the professor remarks, "A more successful captain was Henry Shreve of the *Washington*, which started its runs around 1815. Shreve took his steamboat for a 1,400-mile trip, which took about three weeks."

17 Understanding Function Question

Ⓑ In talking about how quickly the same trip was made years later, the professor implies that engineering improved a great deal during that period of time.

ACTUAL TEST 07

p.117

Answers

PART 1

1. Ⓑ 2. Ⓒ 3. Ⓐ 4. Ⓐ
5. Ⓓ 6. Ⓒ 7. Ⓐ, Ⓒ
8. Hyenas: ②, ④ Vultures: ①, ③ 9. Ⓐ
10. Ⓓ 11. Ⓒ

PART 2

1. Ⓑ, Ⓓ 2. Ⓐ 3. Ⓑ 4. Ⓒ
5. Ⓒ 6. Ⓑ 7. Ⓑ 8. Ⓑ
9. Ⓒ
10. Step 1: Ⓓ Step 2: Ⓒ Step 3: Ⓐ Step 4: Ⓑ
11. Ⓐ 12. Ⓑ
13. Continental Ice Sheets: ② Ice Caps: ④ Ice Fields: ①, ③
14. Ⓑ 15. Ⓐ, Ⓓ 16. Ⓐ 17. Ⓑ

Scripts & Explanations

PART 1 Conversation 🎧 07-01 p.119

M Student: Professor Horace, you don't happen to be too busy at the moment, do you? I wonder if it would be possible to speak with you right now, please.

W Professor: Of course, Sebastian. I already finished both of my classes for the day, so I have plenty of time. What would you like to talk about? The lecture we had in yesterday's class? That was difficult material, so I often get students who ask me about it each semester.

M: Actually, uh, I'd like to discuss the paper I'm going to write for the independent study course I'm taking with you next semester.

W: Ah, so you'd like to get a head start on the work during summer vacation, right?

M: Exactly.

W: That's impressive. You can probably get a lot of research done over the next couple of months if you just spend an hour or two working each day.

M: That's what I'm planning to do. The only problem is, uh, I'm just not sure what my topic should be. I was hoping you could help me out.

W: All right. Let's do a bit of thinking together. What area of archaeology interests you the most?

M: Hmm . . . I really enjoy both the archaeology of Central America as well as that of Egypt. Which of those two do you think I should focus on?

W: Well, as you know, my specialty is Central America, so you'll likely benefit more by focusing on that region since I'll be able to provide you with more assistance. I mean, uh, I know about ancient Egypt, but I'm much more comfortable with Aztec and Mayan archaeology. I can also do some Greek and Roman archaeology if that's what you're interested in.

M: I'm not particularly interested in European archaeology. I think I'd prefer to go with archaeology in Central America.

W: Okay.

M: So, uh, what aspect of Central American archaeology should I look at?

W: Hold on a minute . . . I don't think we can determine something like that right now.

M: Huh? We can't? Why not?

W: Think about it, Sebastian. There are so many different topics which you can examine in this one region. For instance, you could study a specific temple, a dig site, an aspect of cultural archaeology, or many other topics. Instead, what about this . . . ? I'm going to give you a list of five books I'd like you to read before summer vacation begins. They are all going to be general books about the topic you just selected. Once you read them, come back here and speak to me. You can tell me what in the books interested you the most, and then we can come up with a topic.

M: Hmm . . . ⁵That's sounds good, but . . .

W: But what?

M: The semester is almost over, and I've got to study for my final exams. **Five books might be a bit heavy.**

W: Oh, sure. That makes sense. In that case, I'll only give you three. Can you handle that?

M: Definitely. I can do that.

W: Great. Let me get a pen and a piece of paper so that I can write down the titles then.

1 Gist-Purpose Question

Ⓑ The student says, "I'd like to discuss the paper I'm going to write for the independent study course I'm taking with you next semester."

2 Detail Question

Ⓒ The student remarks, "I think I'd prefer to go with archaeology in Central America."

3 Understanding Attitude Question

Ⓐ During the conversation, the professor is very helpful to the student as she suggests various ideas to him.

4 Making Inference Question

Ⓐ At the end of the conversation, the professor states, "Let me get a pen and a piece of paper so that I can write down the titles then."

5 Understanding Function Question

Ⓓ In stating, "Five books might be a bit heavy," the student means that he might not have enough time to read five books because he needs to study for his final exams.

PART 1 Lecture 🎧 07-02   p.122

W Professor: We all know about predators and prey animals, but there is another group, uh, a third group, of animals, which also plays an important role in food systems. I'm talking, of course, about scavengers. A scavenger is an organism that consumes dead or dying organisms. These organisms could have died from natural causes or could have been killed by other animals. As a general rule, scavengers have keen eyesight and hearing plus a strong sense of smell, which enables them to discover dead animals from far away. They also have strong digestive systems which are highly acidic, so they are protected from any diseases or pathogens the dead animals that they consume may be carrying. Let me give you a few examples of scavengers. Hmm . . . There are vultures and hyenas on land, crabs, lobsters, and sharks in the oceans, and numerous species of insects.

M Student: I'm sorry, but I thought hyenas are hunters.

W: You are correct. Hyenas are predators. However, hyenas are also what are known as opportunistic scavengers, which, uh, which means that when given the opportunity, they will consume dead animals. Hyenas typically hunt in packs in order to take down gazelles, warthogs, or other prey. Many other predators, including wolves, lions, and polar bears, are also opportunistic predators. You see, um, very rarely will predators pass up the opportunity for a free meal. Now, hyenas have a reputation as being sneaky thieves that will wait for a lion or a cheetah to kill an animal and then barge in on that predator in great numbers to steal the meal. Sure, that happens, but hyenas also hunt on their own. Nevertheless, they have evolved to be prime scavengers. Their bite is so strong that it can crack the bones of dead animals to give them access to the marrow inside.

Vultures, of which there are a variety of species, are another well-known scavenger. Vultures are almost exclusively scavengers so do not hunt on their own. Because of that, their beaks and talons are typically weaker than those of birds of prey such as eagles and hawks. Yet they are still strong enough to rip the flesh off dead animals. People often see vultures circling in the sky, which indicates that a dead animal is directly below. Vultures have a powerful sense of smell and excellent eyesight, both of which enable them to find dead animals from a distance. They sometimes land near a pride of lions consuming their prey and then wait for the lions to finish, whereupon they move in and consume the leftovers. Sometimes they don't even wait but stay at the edges of the pride and grab what food they can. When the lions depart, the vultures cover the carcass and devour it.

Vultures have evolved in various ways to benefit them as scavengers. Most are bald headed, which helps protect them from bacteria. Some carcasses are covered with toxic bacteria, so vultures consume them with their beaks. Since vultures have bald heads, there are no hairs or feathers for bacteria to stick to. Vultures also have a special way of obtaining food. They find carcasses with only bones remaining. They clutch the bones in their talons, fly high in the sky, drop the bones on the rocks, and then eat the marrow in the bones that crack open.

There are a large number of marine scavengers. In the oceans, many marine species are known to consume the bodies of dead animals such as whales. When a large whale dies, its body soon begins to rot, and the smell attracts sharks and other marine predators. Then, as the carcass falls apart, it starts sinking all the way to the ocean floor, creating what is known as marine snow. In shallow water, marine snow attracts a large number of scavengers, particularly crabs and lobsters. Have you ever wondered how fishermen catch them in lobster pots? Well, they bait the pots with dead fish, and the smell attracts both crabs and lobster. Once they go inside, they can consume the fish, but they wind up trapped and can't escape.

Now, uh, how about insects . . . ? Many species, such as blowflies, consume the last remains of dead animals after both predators and scavengers have moved on. These insects are called decomposers, and they help speed along the process of breaking down the remains of dead animals. This is the last stage in what is a necessary role in ecosystems. You see, uh, scavengers play a key role in their ecosystems in two main ways. The first is that they help remove potential disease-causing elements from their ecosystems. The second is that they help break down the dead and decomposing flesh and bones of dead animals, which enables nutrients to enter the soil. This, in turn, helps plants grow, and as we all know, plants are the foundation of the food system.

6 Gist-Content Question

Ⓒ The professor mostly talks about the various types of scavengers and their consumption methods.

7 Detail Question

Ⓐ, Ⓒ The professor says, "As a general rule, scavengers have keen eyesight and hearing plus a strong sense of smell, which enables them to discover dead animals from far away. They also have strong digestive systems which are highly acidic, so they are protected from any diseases or pathogens the dead animals that they consume may be carrying."

8 Connecting Content Question

Hyenas: ②, ④ Vultures: ①, ③

About hyenas, the professor states, "Hyenas typically hunt in packs in order to take down gazelles, warthogs, or other prey," and adds, "Their bite is so strong that it can crack the bones of dead animals to give them access to the marrow inside." Regarding vultures, the professor comments, "Some carcasses are covered with toxic bacteria, so vultures consume them with their beaks. Since vultures have bald heads, there are no hairs or feathers for bacteria to stick to," and states, "Sometimes they don't even wait but stay at the edges of the pride and grab what food they can."

9 Understanding Organization Question

Ⓐ The professor focuses on how marine snow is created in stating, "In the oceans, many marine species are known to consume the bodies of dead animals such as whales. When a large whale dies, its body soon begins to rot, and the smell attracts sharks and other marine predators. Then, as the carcass falls apart, it starts sinking all the way to the ocean floor, creating what is known as marine snow."

10 Understanding Function Question

Ⓓ The professor tells the students about fishermen to explain how they catch crabs and lobsters with marine snow.

11 Detail Question

Ⓒ The professor notes, "You see, uh, scavengers play a key role in their ecosystems in two main ways. The first is that they help remove potential disease-causing elements from their ecosystems."

PART 2 Conversation 🎧 07-03   p.125

M Librarian: Yes, uh, who is next, please?

W Student: Hi. Um, I have a few questions for you. I'd like to renew this stack of books if it's possible. I believe some of them are late, but I don't know which ones.

M: Wow. That's a monster stack of books. Let me begin to scan them for you to see what the damage is. Our policy is twenty-five cents a day for the first two weeks, and after that, you have to pay for the book. You used to just have to return it and pay five dollars.

W: Wow. That's pretty strict, isn't it? Some of the books are really expensive, aren't they?

M: Well, I don't make the policy. The school does, but to be honest, students have been keeping books out way too long over the past few months without ever returning them. Other students need those books, too, so the university made the penalties stricter in the hope that students will change their habits when it comes to checking out and returning books.

W: Oh, I see. Well, I don't think any of these have been out that long.

M: Okay, uh, I just finished. Actually, all six of them are overdue. Two by two days and four by five days. Your grand total of library fines equals . . . Uh, let me see . . . I need to do a little mental math here . . . Um, six dollars.

W: Um, do you know what? I don't have any cash with me right now. Can you just charge it to my university account?

M: Sure. No problem. Done. Now, you said that you wanted to renew a few of these?

W: That's right. I'd like to keep the two books on historical criticism for another week if I could.

M: Okay. Let me just make sure they have not been reserved or requested by another student or professor. You see, sometimes when a book is out, someone will reserve it because he needs it for a paper or class or something. In that case, I'll have to keep the book for that person, and then you can get it later.

W: Oh, I understand. I've done that before.

M: Whoops. Bad news. Both of the ones you want to renew have been requested by a professor. I'm afraid I'm going to have to hold them.

W: ⁵Oh, no. I've just got to have those two books. I have a huge history paper due on Monday, and those two books are critical to the research I am doing. I mean, without them, there's no way I can write my paper. **I'm dead.** I can't believe this.

M: Hang on now. All is not lost. I can check on the system to see if the junior college library has them. If it does, I can reserve them for you, and then you can run over there and pick them up really quickly.

W: Oh, that would be great. Thanks a lot.

M: Yep, the library there has got both of them. I'm not surprised. Most junior college students wouldn't need books like those. And I've reserved them in your name. So just drop by any time after noon today, and you can get them and check them out.

W: Great. Thanks so much. See you!

1 **Gist-Content Question**

Ⓑ, Ⓓ The speakers are mainly talking about fines the student must pay for overdue books as well as some books the student wants to renew.

2 **Detail Question**

Ⓐ The man says, "Our policy is twenty-five cents a day for the first two weeks, and after that, you have to pay for the book."

3 **Detail Question**

Ⓑ The man tells the student, "The school does, but to be honest, students have been keeping books out way too long over the past few months without ever returning them. Other students need those books, too, so the university made the penalties stricter in the hope that students will change their habits when it comes to checking out and returning books."

4 **Making Inferences Question**

Ⓒ The man reserves two books at the junior college library for the student, so she will probably go there next to check the books out.

5 **Understanding Function Question**

Ⓒ When the student says, "I'm dead," she means that the books are the basis for her homework, but since she cannot have them, she is in trouble.

PART 2 Lecture #1 🎧 07-04   p.128

W Professor: Yes, satellites are one-way communications that are linked together, whether it is cell phones or the Internet or television. But are there any other ways that people are connected? What I mean is . . . how else do we connect the continents and islands of the world? What is another factor of globalization? Well, today there are literally hundreds of cables lying across nearly every ocean floor, all of which connect us with one another. For instance, they connect Japan with the United States and, uh, India with the Maldives. I mean, there are cables all over the place passing information, bank transactions, e-mail, web searches, and just about anything else that you could possibly think of. Many cables even transport gas and oil between continents, not just megabytes.

But what I'd like to talk to you about today is how exactly these cables are laid and the process behind them. It takes special ships, called cable ships, and massive high-tech machines to lay and bury the cables under the ocean floor, and they are always out there, working, laying, and burying cables to make our world more well-connected, efficient, and reliable. So if there aren't any questions at this point, I'll begin to discuss the process.

There are two main vehicles involved in laying oceanic cables. They are cable ships, which I just mentioned, and trenchers, which are complex machines that dig the trenches for the cables, lay the cables in the correct positions, and then finally bury the cables. But before a trencher can even begin, engineers on a cable ship must conduct a survey of the ocean floor to plot the best route for the cable and to look out for hazards. So the cable ship first launches a robotic submarine to take pictures of the seafloor and to check for potential problems, such as rocks, reefs, and even sunken ships or planes. You know, uh, basically anything that would obstruct the cable. The robotic submarine is crucial for the engineers on the cable ship to plot an efficient, obstacle-free path for the oceanic cable. Is everyone still with me . . . ? Excellent.

So, um, once the crew is satisfied with the pathway, they lower the trencher into the water from the cable ship. The trencher is an unmanned vehicle that is maneuvered by a computer. It has a very long umbilical cord connecting it to the cable ship. The cable ship then begins to lead the cable off of the deck, and the trencher follows it to the floor of the ocean. The trencher moves either with tank-like treads on hard soil or skis when it's on more unstable sediment. In the back of the trencher, there are ten fan thrusters that propel it through the water. The next step for the trencher is to dig the actual trench, which it does by using water. It sucks in seawater and blasts it out of the high-pressure nozzles that are attached to its two arms, which swing on the outside of the cable itself. [11] The jet nozzles blow away the seabed, ultimately forming a trench that is typically around six feet deep. The cable then rests comfortably in this. **The consistency of the ocean floor determines what type of blast the trencher uses.** If the ocean floor is sandy, it uses low, even pressure water flow, but if it is hard, a high, intense pressure stream will carve right into it. Today's trenchers are simply enormous machines. They weigh about twenty-five tons and are powered by engines with eight hundred horsepower. They can also dive to depths reaching nearly five thousand feet. Okay, now, next the trencher clears the slush with a vacuum and pumps it out of pipes on the side. This empties the trench and allows the cable to sink into the freshly dug trench.

M Student: I'm sorry, but, uh, I'm a little confused. Why doesn't the cable just float away? Cables are usually hollow, correct?

W: That's a very astute question. Actually, before the crew members spool the cable off the deck of the ship, they begin to fill it with heavy liquids so that what you mentioned won't happen. So at this point, the cable is down in place. Next, the cable ship crew will pull the trencher back up to the surface and outfit it with a burying apparatus. Obviously, this is to bury the cable inside the trench. Now outfitted with a backfill tool, the trencher again descends to the ocean floor and begins to bury the cable with, again, water jets. There are two jets that are used. One blasts the bottom of the trench wall while the other blasts the top of it. Eventually, the trench will collapse on itself and bury the cable completely. At this point, the process is, for the most part, complete, and the cable ship will move on to repeat the process and lay another segment of cable.

6 Gist-Content Question

Ⓑ The professor spends most of the lecture discussing how oceanic cables are planted in the ocean floor.

7 Making Inferences Question

Ⓑ The professor says, "It takes special ships, called cable ships, and massive high-tech machines to lay and bury the cables under the ocean floor." In addition, the professor discusses various types of advanced technology needed throughout the entire lecture.

8 Detail Question

Ⓑ The professor talks about how the trencher uses water to remove soil and sediment from the ocean floor.

9 Detail Question

Ⓒ The professor says, "Actually, before the crew members spool the cable off the deck of the ship, they begin to fill it with heavy liquids so that what you mentioned won't happen."

10 Connecting Content Question

Step 1: Ⓓ   Step 2: Ⓒ   Step 3: Ⓐ   Step 4: Ⓑ

First, the professor says, "But before a trencher can even begin, engineers on a cable ship must conduct a survey of the ocean floor to plot the best route for the cable and to look out for hazards." Next, the professor states, "So, um, once the crew is satisfied with the pathway, they lower the trencher into the water from the cable ship." Then, the professor says, "The cable ship then begins to lead the cable off of the deck, and the trencher follows it to the floor of the ocean." Last, the professor notes, "The next step for the trencher is to dig the actual trench, which it does by using water."

11 Understanding Function Question

Ⓐ In stating, "The consistency of the ocean floor determines what type of blast the trencher uses," the professor implies that the makeup of the ocean floor varies.

PART 2 Lecture #2 🎧 07-05   p.131

W Professor: Okay, uh, do you have any more questions, or shall I move on to the next topic . . . ? Great. It looks like everyone is fine with me continuing the lecture. The next topic I wish to discuss is glaciers. I'm sure you are all aware that glaciers are enormous sheets of ice which are capable of moving. When that happens, despite being solid in structure, they move as if they were liquid since they essentially flow in a downhill direction. But what I bet the majority of you are unaware of is that there are actually multiple types of glaciers. Right now, I'd like to discuss a few of those with you.

The first three types of glaciers about which I would like to inform you are rather similar to one another. I'm talking about continental ice sheets, ice caps, and ice fields. Let me go over them according to their sizes. Continental ice sheets, as the name implies, are gargantuan glaciers covering entire landscapes . . . uh, continents even. There are two in existence today. One is in Antarctica and covers more than 5.4 million square miles of land. As a way of comparison, that is approximately the size of both the United States and Mexico combined. And just so you know how huge this sheet really is, in some places in Antarctica, the ice is more than three miles thick. Greenland, an enormous island that sits between North America and Europe in the North Atlantic Ocean, is another continental ice sheet as a glacier covers nearly the entire island.

M Student: Professor Roth, there are only two today, but were there more in the past, such as during one of the ice ages?

W: You figured that one out quickly, Matt. Yes, during the last ice age, there was a continental ice sheet that covered most of the land which is modern-day Canada and parts of the United States. In addition, other continental ice sheets covered many parts of Europe and also Siberia.

Let's move on to ice caps. They are pretty much the same as continental ice sheets except for one thing. They cover an area fewer than 20,000 square miles. That's still a very large amount of land, and ice caps are capable of covering entire mountain ranges. There's an ice cap in Iceland that occupies nearly ten percent of the entire island. Interestingly enough, that ice cap covers several active volcanoes. When they erupt, glacier ice melts in large quantities, which can cause severe flooding. As for ice fields, they are similar to ice caps. However, ice caps look like domes, which allows them to shape the land itself. Ice fields, on the other hand, tend to be flat. As a result, they are incapable of covering mountains. What might happen is that they occupy land in the valleys between individual mountains, but the mountain peaks rise above the ice fields. These, as you can guess, are much more common than both continental ice shelves and ice caps. There are ice fields in the Himalayas in Asia as well as in the Alps in Europe. In North America, there are some ice fields in the Rocky Mountains.

Many of these enormous glaciers have other types of glaciers attached to them. One of these is called an ice stream. As the name implies, ice streams are capable of moving fast. Some can move more than 3,200 feet per year. Ice streams move much, much faster than other types of glaciers. Yes, Matt?

M: What makes them move so fast?

W: There are several reasons. One is that they are frequently outlets to the ocean for larger glaciers. Basically, uh, they drain parts of glaciers. This means they can be very long, thick, and wide. How big are they? Some can be hundreds of miles long, up to thirty miles wide, and more than one mile thick. Ice streams tend to form downhill since they go to the ocean or sea, so the slope downward toward the sea can help them move quickly. Additionally, liquid water sometimes follows the same paths as ice streams, which makes the ice above it move faster. Finally, ice streams may contain various types of sediment, which makes them capable of moving quickly.

Another type of glacier similar to ice streams is an outlet glacier. It too moves downhill and can help drain some large ice sheets. However, outlet glaciers tend to form in gaps between mountains. As a result, the solid rock on both sides prevents them from widening very much.

Now, uh . . . Oh, it looks like we've just run out of time. That's too bad because I need to tell you about some other glaciers, including hanging glaciers and rock glaciers. I guess I'll have to do that in our next class. All right, everyone. Please remember to finish reading chapter five in your textbooks by Thursday. I'll see you then.

12 Gist-Content Question

Ⓑ The professor mostly discusses different types of glaciers in her lecture.

13 Connecting Content Question

Continental Ice Sheets: ② Ice Caps: ④ Ice Fields: ①, ③
About continental ice sheets, the professor states, "Continental ice sheets, as the name implies, are gargantuan glaciers covering entire landscapes . . . uh, continents even. There are two in existence today." Regarding ice caps, she notes, "Ice caps are capable of covering entire mountain ranges." As for ice fields, she remarks, "Ice fields, on the other hand, tend to be flat," and adds, "There are ice fields in the Himalayas in Asia."

14 Understanding Attitude Question

Ⓑ In stating, "You figured that one out quickly, Matt," in response to the student's comment, the professor shows that she is impressed with the way the student thinks.

15 Detail Question

Ⓐ, Ⓓ The professor says, "Liquid water sometimes follows the same paths as ice streams, which makes the ice above it move faster. Finally, ice streams may contain various types of sediment, which makes them capable of moving quickly."

16 Making Inferences Question

Ⓐ The professor states, "It too moves downhill and can help drain some large ice sheets. However, outlet glaciers tend to form in gaps between mountains. As a result, the solid rock on both sides prevents them from widening very much." It can therefore be inferred that outlet glaciers are not as wide as ice streams.

17 Understanding Function Question

Ⓑ The professor gives the students a homework assignment in stating, "Please remember to finish reading chapter five in your textbooks by Thursday."

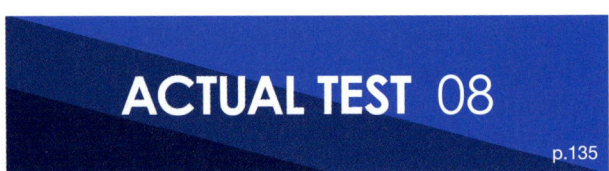

ACTUAL TEST 08

p.135

Answers

PART 1

1 Ⓒ   2 Ⓒ   3 Ⓑ, Ⓒ   4 Ⓑ
5 Ⓐ   6 Ⓒ   7 Ⓐ   8 Ⓒ
9 Ⓒ   10 Ⓐ   11 Ⓐ, Ⓓ   12 Ⓑ
13 Ⓓ   14 Ⓒ   15 Ⓒ
16 National Parks: ①, ② National Monuments: ③, ④
17 Ⓐ

PART 2

1 Ⓒ   2 Ⓐ, Ⓓ   3 Ⓒ   4 Ⓐ
5 Ⓓ   6 Ⓒ   7 Ⓓ   8 Ⓐ
9 Ⓑ   10 Ⓑ, Ⓓ   11 Ⓒ

Scripts & Explanations

PART 1 Conversation 🎧 08-01　　　　　　　　p.137

M Student: Professor Propst, have you had an opportunity to review my paper yet? I was hoping to get your comments so that I could look at them tonight and make any changes you suggest. That way, uh, I can turn my midterm paper in ahead of time.

W Professor: [5] Yes, Larry, I have just finished going over the paper.

M: That's wonderful. Could I please have it?

W: I think you'd better have a seat for a moment.

M: Oh . . . You didn't like it?

W: Hmm . . . I wouldn't say that. On the contrary, I thought the general thesis of your paper was rather creative. But there are a few parts I believe we need to discuss. You're not busy right now, are you?

M: Well, I have class with Professor Wellborn in about thirty minutes. You're, uh, you're not going to keep me here for that long, are you?

W: No, I don't think so. This should only require a couple of minutes.

M: That's a relief. Okay, uh, then let's do this now if you don't mind.

W: Great. So . . . here is your paper.

M: Hmm . . . That's a lot of red ink.

W: Well, I made many comments because I am confident that you can do a better job. Let's look at this together . . . Now, uh, as you can see, I made some positive comments about your introduction. I thought you stated your thesis very well. You wrote exactly what you believe and what you hope to prove in the rest of your essay.

M: Thanks. So what did I do wrong then?

W: Basically, you didn't make good arguments in your body paragraphs. Take a look at the argument in your first paragraph . . . Look at this sentence here. It actually goes against your thesis statement. You just disproved what your thesis is about.

M: Oh . . . I did, didn't I?

W: So you either need to come up with an entirely new thesis, which is something I would prefer you not do, or you should delete the first paragraph and make a new argument.

M: I'll go with the latter choice.

W: Outstanding. I thought you would see it that way. Now, uh, let's go to the second page. Here in this paragraph, I don't believe this quotation you included means what you think it means. Why don't you try reading it again to make sure you really understand it? And look here on the last page . . . Your conclusion makes a different argument than your introduction. You simply cannot do that.

M: Okay. I see exactly what you're talking about. Is there anything else?

W: Two more things. You have three or four grammar mistakes and a couple of spelling errors in your paper. That's pure carelessness. In this day of spell checkers and grammar checkers, there is no excuse for making simple mistakes like that. Please be sure to clean up those errors before you turn in your paper for real. Okay?

M: Yes, ma'am. Well, my original plan was to submit the paper tomorrow, but I don't think that's going to happen. I'll try to get it to you by the end of the week.

W: That will still be one week early, so your schedule is perfectly fine.

M: Thanks a lot, Professor. I really appreciate the time you took to go over this for me.

1　Gist-Content Question

Ⓒ At the beginning of the conversation, the student says, "Professor Propst, have you had an opportunity to review my paper yet? I was hoping to get your comments so that I could look at them tonight and make any changes you suggest."

2　Gist-Purpose Question

Ⓒ The professor comments, "Now, uh, as you can see, I made some positive comments about your introduction. I thought you stated your thesis very well. You wrote exactly what you believe and what you hope to prove in the rest of your essay."

3　Detail Question

Ⓑ, Ⓒ First, the professor notes, "Basically, you didn't make good arguments in your body paragraphs." Then, the professor adds, "You have three or four grammar mistakes and a couple of spelling errors in your paper."

4　Making Inference Question

Ⓑ After the student says that he will try to turn the paper in this week, the professor responds, "That will still be one week early, so your schedule is perfectly fine." So it can be inferred that the paper must be turned in sometime next week.

5　Understanding Function Question

Ⓐ When the student asks to have his paper back and the professor responds, "I think you'd better have a seat for a moment," the professor is implying that she wants to talk to the student about his paper.

PART 1 Lecture #1 08-02 p.140

M Professor: An additional aspect of the sun's corona is something that we call solar wind. This is a mass of ejected protons and electrons in the form of plasma and that speeds away from the sun at high speeds. The speeds fluctuate from around 400 kilometers per second around the sun's equator to approximately 700 kilometers per second near the sun's poles. This cluster of particles spreads throughout the solar system, where its mass is typically deflected by planetary bodies such as Earth. Solar wind does, however, have certain effects on our planet, which I'm going to describe in detail after I first tell you how we discovered solar wind.

In the nineteenth century and the early twentieth century, astronomers in Europe and the United States noticed various phenomena associated with the sun. These included increased brightness of the sun due to what we now know are solar flares. This was then followed by an increase in geomagnetic activity on the Earth. These astronomers theorized that the sun was so hot that much of its heat was carried in the corona, whose limits had to extend far out into space . . . even beyond Earth's orbit. Additionally, many astronomers noted that the tails of comets always pointed away from the sun as they passed through the solar system, so they theorized that something about the sun was causing this phenomenon. In 1957, American astronomer Eugene Parker suggested that all of these things were the result of what he called solar wind, the high-speed movement of electrons and protons from the corona of the sun.

Parker's theory was based on the temperature of the plasma of the corona, which at the time was believed to be around two million degrees Celsius. Parker theorized that the plasma was so hot that the sun's gravity could no longer hold it in place; therefore, it was ejected into space in the form of waves of plasma carrying protons and electrons.

W Student: Was Parker's theory accepted by other astronomers?

M: Not initially, but over the years, uh, other astronomers examined his mathematical calculations and found nothing wrong with them. Still, there wasn't tangible proof until there was an increase in space probe launches from the Earth during the early 1960s. First Russian and later American space probes discovered evidence of solar wind, so Parker's theory was finally accepted as fact.

Now, let me examine solar wind in more detail. Generally, there's a constant flow of plasma from the sun's corona into space. There are two types of solar wind, which we call slow solar wind and fast solar wind.

As I mentioned earlier, slow solar wind originates around the sun's equator while fast solar wind forms closer to the poles. The reason for this is the formation of coronal holes, which are cooler regions near the poles. The cooler temperatures allow the plasma in the corona more easily to escape and to move at higher speeds than the plasma at the equator. There are also sometimes massive increases in the amount of solar wind. These are typically caused by what we call coronal mass ejections, or solar flares, which are huge flares of ejected material from the corona. During these ejections, solar wind can attain speeds of up to 1,000 kilometers per second.

So, uh, what about the effects that solar wind has on Earth and the rest of the solar system? As solar wind approaches planetary bodies that have strong magnetic fields, such as Earth, then it is deflected around these bodies. You see, um, Earth's magnetic field is like a bubble that protects it. It's called the magnetosphere. It's generally believed that without the magnetosphere, the planet would have no life as we know it. The magnetosphere protects the Earth—especially its atmosphere—from solar wind and other harmful cosmic rays. Mars, unlike Earth, has no life and a very thin atmosphere, which astronomers believe was mostly stripped away by solar wind millions of years ago.

One thing to note is that not all particles from solar wind are deflected, so some enter the upper atmosphere. One noticeable effect of that is the increased brightness of auroras in the polar regions in the Northern and Southern hemispheres. If the solar wind is strong enough, auroras can also be seen far from the poles. During coronal mass ejections, powerful solar wind can hit the Earth and influence the atmosphere and the magnetic field. Satellites circling the planet can suffer damage and disruptions to their orbits as well. When powerful storms hit, astronauts on the International Space Station remain inside and avoid doing spacewalks. On the ground, navigation systems using GPS technology may be disrupted. Power grids may also be affected by solar wind storms, so there could be disruptions to telephone and Internet services on some occasions. Obviously, powerful solar wind can be harmful in a number of ways.

6 Gist-Content Question

Ⓒ The professor mainly discusses the discovery and effects of solar wind.

7 Understanding Organization Question

Ⓐ The professor covers the information about the discovery of solar wind by talking about it in chronological order.

8 Understanding Organization Question

Ⓒ The professor discusses Parker's theory in stating, "In 1957, American astronomer Eugene Parker suggested that all of these things were the result of what he called solar wind, the high-speed movement of electrons and protons from the corona of the sun. Parker's theory was based on the temperature of the plasma of the corona, which at the time was believed to be around two million degrees Celsius. Parker theorized that the plasma was so hot that the sun's gravity could no longer hold it in place; therefore, it was ejected into space in the form of waves of plasma carrying protons and electrons."

9 Connecting Content Question

Ⓒ First, the professor says, "The speeds fluctuate from around 400 kilometers per second around the sun's equator to approximately 700 kilometers per second near the sun's poles." Then, he states, "Slow solar wind originates around the sun's equator." So it can be inferred that slow solar wind travelers around 400 kilometers per second.

10 Making Inferences Question

Ⓐ The professor notes, "The magnetosphere protects the Earth—especially its atmosphere—from solar wind and other harmful cosmic rays. Mars, unlike Earth, has no life and a very thin atmosphere, which astronomers believe was mostly stripped away by solar wind millions of years ago." It can therefore be inferred that Mars has no magnetosphere.

11 Detail Question

Ⓐ, Ⓓ The professor remarks, "On the ground, navigation systems using GPS technology may be disrupted. Power grids may also be affected by solar wind storms, so there could be disruptions to telephone and Internet services on some occasions."

PART 1 Lecture #2 🎧 08-03   p.143

M Professor: There is an act that presidents have relied on in the past to promote both the interests of the United States as well as their own. It is called the Antiquities Act. It was signed by Theodore Roosevelt in 1906, and it gives the president the power basically to block off public land owned by the U.S. government and to declare it off limits to private enterprise and development. Let me try to state this a bit more clearly. The Antiquities Act gives the president the unobstructed power to designate land as national monuments, usually for conservation purposes. And since its onset, at least eighteen presidents have used it.

W Student: But what about Congress? Doesn't it have a role?

M: Well, this has been the main issue people have with the act. Congress has little to no power in controlling what a president deems an antiquity and designates as a national monument. Now, let me make this distinction clear, everyone. Congress does have within its power the ability to designate and name national parks. Parks, everyone, not monuments. The president, on the other hand, has the sole power to use the Antiquities Act to designate national monuments. We must make sure we separate the two. For example, Yellowstone National Park, the first national park in the United States as well as the entire world, for that matter, was established by Congress, in the year 1872.

Another distinguishing factor between national parks and national monuments is the speed with which they can be created. In the case of parks, Congress must write and ratify the declaration much like a law. It must be accepted and agreed upon by both houses and then, finally, implemented. This, of course, can take years to accomplish in some instances. The process can be quite long and drawn out. On the other hand, monuments are at the president's discretion only. They can be established whenever the president feels like creating one. Once determined, little can be done to retract or stop the establishment of monuments. Does everyone have a good handle on what I have discussed so far?

W: Why did the government come up with the Antiquities Act in the first place, sir?

M: Well, I believe the answer to your question is complex, but I'll give it a shot. [17] I think it represents the idealism prevalent in the United States in the early twentieth century. Presidents wanted the ability to preserve the vast natural resources and land of the country. They wanted future generations to enjoy and benefit from what existed at the time in its unadulterated version. **They also realized the potential for some places to be exploited in the future.** In many ways, the future vision of the act and the conservational theme as well as of the presidents themselves is quite honorable. In essence, it was an attempt to preserve and protect land for future generations. It was also established to remind future generations to appreciate and respect the world around them and to serve as a warning not to destroy it. I mean . . . the vision of the early presidents as well as recent ones, everyone, in establishing national monuments is perhaps the one remaining good thing which links them together. You know, uh, this sense of responsibility of preservation.

W: Professor, which national monument was the first to be established under the Antiquities Act?

M: Just a few months after the act was enacted, Roosevelt named Devil's Tower in the state of Wyoming the first national monument. A couple of years after that, he established the protection of nearly one million acres of the Grand Canyon because, as he said, it was "an object of unusual scientific interest." Another famous monument that resulted from the act is, of course, the Statue of Liberty, which received its status thirty-eight years after it was presented to the country by France. You would have thought they would not have taken that long to establish the Statue of Liberty, wouldn't you?

Moving up in history, it seems that President Bill Clinton was the most prolific user of the Antiquities Act. In 1996, he used his power for the first time to establish Utah's Grand Staircase, Escalante, as a national monument. Five years later, just before he left office, Clinton managed to designate seven other national monuments to be reminders of his legacy. With the establishment of these final seven, Clinton's grand total of national monuments came to nineteen. That's a lot, huh? In addition, in 2006, George W. Bush got into the act by establishing the Northwestern Hawaii Islands Marine National Monument, which protects all of the islands extending westward to the Midway Islands. Well, that's about all the time we have today, everyone. Please read up on how the Antiquities Act was used by President Carter in Alaska and the issues that arose from it for your homework.

12 Gist-Content Question

Ⓑ The professor mostly talks about the Antiquities Act and why it is so important.

13 Making Inferences Question

Ⓒ The professor states, "In the case of parks, Congress must write and ratify the declaration much like a law. It must be accepted and agreed upon by both houses and then, finally, implemented. This, of course, can take years to accomplish in some instances. The process can be quite long and drawn out. On the other hand, monuments are at the president's discretion only. They can be established whenever the president feels like creating one."

14 Detail Question

Ⓒ The professor says, "Just a few months after the act was enacted, Roosevelt named Devil's Tower in the state of Wyoming the first national monument."

15 Detail Question

Ⓒ The professor comments, "Moving up in history, it seems that President Bill Clinton was the most prolific user of the Antiquities Act. In 1996, he used his power for the first time to establish Utah's Grand Staircase, Escalante, as a national monument. Five years later, just before he left office, Clinton managed to designate seven other national monuments to be reminders of his legacy. With the establishment of these final seven, Clinton's grand total of national monuments came to nineteen."

16 Connecting Content Question

National Parks: [1], [2] National Monuments: [3], [4]

About national parks, the professor notes, "Congress does have within its power the ability to designate and name national parks," and adds, "In the case of parks, Congress must write and ratify the declaration much like a law. It must be accepted and agreed upon by both houses and then, finally, implemented. This, of course, can take years to accomplish in some instances." Regarding national monuments, the professor states, "Congress has little to no power in controlling what a president deems an antiquity and designates as a national monument," and also says, "The Antiquities Act gives the president the unobstructed power to designate land as national monuments."

17 Understanding Function Question

Ⓐ In stating, "They also realized the potential for some places to be exploited in the future," the professor implies that students should understand that many U.S. presidents wanted to protect land.

PART 2 Conversation 🎧 08-04   p.146

W Student Activities Employee: Good afternoon and welcome to the student activities office. My name is Leslie Hawkins. How may I be of assistance?

M Student: Hello, Ms. Hawkins. My name is Chad Gordon, and I'm the president of the mathematics club here on campus.

W: Congratulations. Were you just elected this week?

M: Thank you. Yes, I was selected president at the first meeting of the semester last night. So, uh, I thought I would drop by here because . . . well, honestly, I have absolutely no idea what I'm doing, so I thought you might be able to help me.

W: [5] That's exactly what I'm here for. And it's perfectly fine to be confused about your duties. **To be frank, nearly every club president comes by this office at least once a semester.**

M: Well, that makes me feel much better now that I know I'm not alone.

W: Just between you and me . . . you're the third club president to come into my office today, and it's only one thirty. I fully expect another couple of students to drop by before I go home for the day.

M: Huh. So . . . uh, what do I do?

W: All right. Getting started. The first thing you should do is submit a list of members. All university clubs must have at least twelve members, or they will not be recognized by the school. The list should include each student's name, student ID number, and signature.

M: I have that with me right here . . . Uh, here you are . . . As you can see, we have eighteen members.

W: Well, you're on the ball, aren't you? This is the first members list I've received this semester.

M: Is there any other paperwork I need to submit?

W: Not at the moment. Now, um, some clubs meet once a week, but most meet only once every two weeks. I suppose it's up to your members to decide how often you get together. Did you discuss that last night?

M: Yes, we did. We decided to meet once every two weeks. We're hoping to meet every other Tuesday evening from six thirty to eight. I suppose we need to reserve a room. Can you do that?

W: I sure can. I'll find you a room suitable for twenty people in just a bit.

M: Thank you.

W: Now, what about special activities? Do you have any plans to, uh, you know, visit a museum or to go on a trip somewhere?

M: Well, we talked about that, but that's going to cost money, and most of the members are not really financially in a position to spend money on any trips.

W: Oh, I'm so glad you dropped by. I've got great news for you. As a recognized club on campus, you are eligible to have the school sponsor two special events each semester.

M: You're kidding, right?

W: Absolutely not. You are permitted to spend up to seven hundred dollars for each event, which should enable you to cover transportation costs as well as entrance fees. Of course, you need to provide receipts to get everything paid for.

M: Wow. You know . . . You're right. I really am glad I visited you today.

1 Gist-Content Question

ⓒ During the conversation, the speakers mainly talk about what the student can do as the leader of his club.

2 Detail Question

Ⓐ, Ⓓ The woman tells the man, "The first thing you should do is submit a list of members. All university clubs must have at least twelve members, or they will not be recognized by the school. The list should include each student's name, student ID number, and signature."

3 Making Inference Question

ⓒ The woman says, "I'll find you a room suitable for twenty people in just a bit," so it can be inferred that she will reserve a room for the student soon.

4 Understanding Attitude Question

Ⓐ At the end of the conversation, the student says, "I really am glad I visited you today," so he is clearly pleased with the way that the woman assists him.

5 Understanding Function Question

Ⓓ In stating, "To be frank, nearly every club president comes by this office at least once a semester," the woman implies that the presidents of most of the clubs at the school need her help at some point.

PART 2 Lecture 🎧 08-05   p.149

M Professor: Good morning, everyone. Before we get started on today's lecture, let me remind you about your midterm papers. They are due no later than 5:00 this evening. You can print them and then hand them in to me, as many of you have already done, or you can email them to me if you prefer doing that. Please note that I will not accept any late papers, so you must get them to me within the next few hours. Does everyone understand . . . ? Wonderful.

In our last class, I spoke about the Neolithic Age. If you will recall, the Paleolithic Age, uh, the Old Stone Age, came first, and it was then followed by the Neolithic Age. That term, of course, means the New Stone Age. That was a time when humans used stones for tools. Well, uh, humanity made a huge leap forward when it next moved into the Bronze Age. This, as you can surmise, was when humans began using bronze to make tools and weapons. Bronze is an alloy comprised of a combination of copper and tin.

W Student: I'm sorry for the interruption, sir, but when did the Bronze Age begin?

M: It depends.

W: It depends? Depends on what?

M: It depends upon which geographical area you're referring to. You see, uh, different cultures discovered— or were introduced to—the ability to create bronze at different times. It wasn't like all of the world's cultures discovered the knowledge simultaneously. Let me see . . . In Greece, the Bronze Age began more than 5,000 years ago before 3000 B.C. The same is true about China. Those were among the two most advanced cultures in ancient times. However, it's almost certain that the first place where the Bronze Age began was the Middle East. The Sumerians were likely the first people to begin working with bronze. Of course, uh, in other places, the Bronze Age started much later. For instance, the Bronze Age didn't start in Britain until around 1900 B.C.

One thing I believe I should point out is that tin and copper, the two components of bronze, are almost never found together in the ground. The only place where they were mined together was Cornwall, which is in the southwestern part of Britain. This means that people in different regions had to mine tin and copper and then transport one to the other. If you ask me, that's surely why the Bronze Age started so late. Ancient cultures simply didn't have the ability to engage in the long-distance trade necessary to acquire the metal which they didn't have access to.

So . . . what were the main features of the Bronze Age? First, obviously, is the use of bronze to make tools and weapons. Second, writing systems began to be developed by some cultures. And third, there was a rise in urbanization during that time. By that, I mean that many people began to abandon their nomadic hunter-gatherer ways and started living in permanent settlements. None of them was a large city like we have today, but there were some urban areas with sizable populations established during that time.

W: Why were so many people able to stop being hunter-gatherers? In our last class, you mentioned that people had already discovered agriculture during the New Stone Age.

M: That's a good observation, Wendy. One of the main reasons is, well, bronze. You see, blacksmiths were able to make farming implements out of bronze. Those were much better and more efficient tools than ones made of stone. Bronze tools enabled farmers to become more productive, which resulted in fewer people being required to farm the land. Some of those excess people then moved to cities, where they could take on other occupations.

W: Oh, I think I get it . . . Is that why some writing systems were created? I mean, uh, people had more time to think and work since they weren't all occupied with getting food.

M: Bingo. That's exactly what happened. Something else that occurred then was that trade routes started to expand during the Bronze Age. People didn't only trade with settlements nearby. Instead, trade routes that covered great distances were established. For instance, tin from Cornwall was traded to people living in the Mediterranean region. That was a tremendous distance at that time. Since trade was expanding, people had to be able to keep accurate records of what was traded and for how much. That was one inducement which encouraged people to create writing systems. They often started as ways to keep track of trade and then later expanded to have other uses.

Ah, I should also mention that both the wheel and the potter's wheel were invented during the Bronze Age. Those two inventions had dramatic effects on the civilizations that used them. Now, I've given you a bit of an overview of this time. Let me go into detail about the period now. I'd like to start with the Sumerian civilization in the Middle East.

6 Gist-Content Question

Ⓒ The professor mainly discusses the primary features of the Bronze Age in his lecture.

7 Understanding Function Question

Ⓓ About the midterm papers, the professor announces, "They are due no later than 5:00 this evening."

8 Making Inferences Question

Ⓐ The professor states, "In Greece, the Bronze Age began more than 5,000 years ago before 3000 B.C. The same is true about China." Then, he adds, "The Sumerians were likely the first people to begin working with bronze." It can therefore be inferred that Sumerians entered the Bronze Age before 3000 B.C.

9 Understanding Organization Question

Ⓑ About Cornwall, the professor notes, "One thing I believe I should point out is that tin and copper, the two components of bronze, are almost never found together in the ground. The only place where they were mined together was Cornwall."

10 Detail Question

Ⓑ, Ⓓ About the Bronze Age, the professor lectures, "Second, writing systems began to be developed by some cultures. And third, there was a rise in urbanization during that time."

11 Understanding Attitude Question

Ⓒ The professor is clearly pleased with the student in how she thinks about people living in the Bronze Age when he states, "Bingo. That's exactly what happened," in response to her comment.